Survivor

ASSISTANCE HANDBOOK

BY MARK COLGAN, CFP®

CFP® and Certified Financial Planner™ are trademarks of the Certified Financial Planner Board of Standards, Inc.

Post It® Notes is a registered trademark of the 3M Company.

Library of Congress Cataloging-in-Publication Data
TX5-700-851
Card Catalog Number: 306.9
Author: Mark Colgan (b. 1970-)
Publisher: Plan Your Legacy, LLC, Pittsford NY,
(585) 419-2272
Paging: 166
ISBN 10: 0-9725356-4-0
ISBN 13: 978-0-9725356-4-9
Notes: Includes glossary and index.
Contents: This fourth edition is a comprehensive guide to the important tasks survivors must do and consider in the hours, days and weeks after the death of a spouse. What makes this edition so powerful is that it includes the insights of many professionals. In addition to my expertise, I welcomed input from an attorney, accountant, grief recovery counselor and two funeral directors.

Subjects:
1. Death-legal and financial aspects–U.S.
2. End-of-life planning–U.S.
3. Legacy planning

Printed and bound in the United States of America.

Dedication

This book is dedicated to my beloved
late wife, Joanne, who gave me
the gift of a wonderful life,
and to survivors everywhere who share
the burden of loss and hope for eternal love.

Contents

Acknowledgements

Although this book was a labor of love, it would not have been possible without the contribution of many good people. Together we shared heartfelt life experiences, professional knowledge and the passion to create a book that helps to significantly ease the burden for many survivors.

First and foremost, I would like to thank the two people who inspired me to write this book—my late wife Joanne and my deceased mother, Bobbi. The courage and kindness Joanne displayed throughout her life was a true motivation for me to embrace life, live it to its fullest and share quality time with people I love. My mother— beyond being an awesome mom—was also a good role model. She always showed a genuine interest in helping others and never asked for recognition, for she knew that the simple pleasure from lending a hand was much more rewarding than any pat on the back.

Needless to say, I deeply appreciate the input from the many people across the country who opened their hearts to share endearing stories of survival. Their heartfelt experiences gave invaluable information to ensure that this book strikes a balance between being practical yet personal.

I am also very thankful for the support of my "dream team." This fourth edition was proofed and edited by the talents of an expert attorney, two accountants, a grief recovery counselor and two funeral directors. This unique approach ensures you are obtaining expert advice from some of the most talented professionals in their fields. Let me share with you a little about each of our contributors.

Our contributing attorney, John ("John A") Warnick became a partner in the Denver office of Holme Roberts & Owen LLP in January, 1999 after practicing in Wyoming and Nevada for twenty years. He is the founder of Family Wealth Transitions and Solutions, a consulting firm that assists clients and their advisory teams in the areas of Purposeful Planning, Trust Design & Implementation. Through his own law practice, John also continues to provide cutting-edge services for the design of multi-generational trusts to minimize transfer taxes and avoid state income taxes. John delivers workshops across the nation for financial planners and attorneys sharing the six paradigms of Purposeful Planning and the Seven Secrets of the Purposeful Trust. To learn more visit, his website at www.johnawarnick.com.

Tony A. Rose, a senior partner of Rose, Snyder & Jacobs, graciously contributed his accounting intelligence. At his firm, he provides tax and management consulting advice to closely-held corporations, family-owned businesses, partnerships and the high net worth individuals that own them. Tony spends a considerable amount of time resolving the complexities faced by families of wealth. Through his counseling and leadership, he has provided valuable guidance on matters where "life intersects wealth."

Jasmin Epstein, our other contributing accountant, is a tax supervisor at the firm of Rose, Snyder & Jacobs. She specializes in estate and gift tax planning, focusing on the personal aspects as well as the financial impacts of family wealth and values transfers. Jasmin earned her undergraduate degree from the University of Illinois at Urbana-Champaign and her Master's degree in Business Taxation from the University of Southern California. She attained her designation as a CPA in 2006.

Russell Friedman has been working with grievers for more than two decades. He has served as a consultant to thousands of bereavement professionals and provides grief recovery seminars and certification programs throughout the United States and Canada. Friedman is co-founder and executive director of the Grief Recovery Institute. He is also the co-author of *The Grief Recovery Handbook*, *When Children Grieve* and *Moving On*.

Stephen Moeller is a licensed funeral director at Floral Haven funeral home in Broken Arrow, OK and has been in the profession since 1978. Interestingly, he also established one of the first Grief Recovery Outreach Programs over 25 years ago. Since then, thousands of grievers have gone through his programs. Steve serves on the Tulsa County Task Force on Infant Mortality and the Tulsa Human Response Coalition and is a member of "Ask the Experts" on Aurora Casket's Funeral Plan.

Scott Anthony, a licensed funeral director since 1982, is Vice-President of the Anthony Funeral & Cremation Chapels of Rochester, NY. He is also an active participant in local, state and national funeral director associations. His primary interest has been to support the funeral industry's effort to protect consumers by promoting ethical and regulatory standards for funeral professionals. He is currently the Chairman of the Funeral Service Foundation, which is the charitable voice of the industry.

Once again, thank you to John A, Tony, Jasmin, Russell, Steve and Scott for your invaluable insight.

A big thanks also goes out to my editor, Cathy Kennedy Godlewski, owner of Write Mind in Rochester, NY. Through her 20 years of copywriting, strategic marketing, and public relations experience, she was able to contribute valuable insight that helped me reshape this fourth edition.

Last but not least, I would like to thank my wife, Kathy. Beyond giving me the opportunity to once again have a wonderful life, her love and support have been a large influence on the continued success of this book.

Note

The information contained in this handbook is intended to serve as a general guide for people dealing with the practical issues that arise from the loss of a loved one. It cannot replace the sound advice of an attorney, accountant, financial planner or other professionals. You should always consult with the appropriate professional before taking any action.

Preface

The loss you have experienced is unique and incomparable to any other. No loss could be worse. Unfortunately, there is no handbook, process, friend or family member that could begin to understand what you are going through; but opening your heart to the people and organizations around you may help you take a step towards grieving fully and making a better future for yourself. Keep an open mind while letting your precious memories sustain you through this difficult period.

My Own Survivor Experience

Joanne and I had an incredible relationship. In addition to having the best friendship anyone could ever ask for, we shared the magic of a loving marriage. It was truly a wonderful life.

In addition to enjoying the fruits of a loving relationship, Joanne and I unfortunately experienced the challenges which life so often brings. One of these challenges, as a result of Joanne's congenital heart disease, was that our lifestyle had to be a bit more relaxed than many. The simple things in life, activities such as going for a walk or shopping at the mall, often had to take a back seat to her fatigue and need for rest. Still, these minor sacrifices were insignificant in comparison to the treasures of the life we shared.

With time, however, Joanne's challenges escalated as her heart complications progressed. In 2000, after just six years of marriage, her condition worsened. When she developed pneumonia, we found ourselves speaking with doctors about heart transplants.

Even though they didn't feel she needed one at the time, we started the application process. Apparently the waiting list was two to five years and their foresight suggested one might be needed within that timeframe. Interestingly, they also stressed that while her condition was critical over the long term, they felt there was no immediate threat to her life.

The year 2001 was a roller coaster. The new year, while marked with optimism for recovery, ended tragically. Toward the end of summer, just when it seemed that Joanne began feeling better, she died suddenly.

On the morning of Tuesday, September 4, after a pleasure-filled weekend with her family at the lake, Joanne passed away. Fortunately, even though we had no idea her death was imminent, our last moments together were very peaceful. Such an experience has taught me to never forget the golden rule—live your life

and love those close to you as if it were your last
day together.

The hours following Joanne's death were dramatic.
Within minutes of her passing, I found myself in the
midst of a crowd of emergency medical technicians,
firemen, policemen, relatives, neighbors and the medical
examiner. Within hours of her death, I was writing her
obituary, selecting her casket, planning the details
surrounding her funeral, purchasing a gravesite for both
of us and even designing her headstone. Within six
hours, I had gone from waking up with my wife to
beginning the process of burying her.

My life was dramatically changed forever. It went from a
wonderful life to one of tremendous, unbearable pain. I
walked a path of introspection and carried on an internal
debate about my purpose in life.

During this most difficult time, I also had to deal with a
mountain of financial details that sprung up quickly.
Some might think that for a Certified Financial Planner™
professional like myself, such details would not be
difficult for me. But, like you, my emotions left little
room for my normal logical and practical thinking.

I remember asking myself, "If this is difficult for me, a
certified financial planner, how does someone who isn't
a financial expert even begin to deal with this?" It was in
this discovery process that I decided to channel my

energy into helping others by writing this book, speaking around the country and establishing Plan Your Legacy, a company dedicated to helping individuals plan meaningful legacies.

By writing this handbook, my goal is to help you navigate the financial and paperwork challenges during one of life's most difficult times. While *The Survivor Assistance Handbook* cannot replace the one-on-one consulting that I often provide to survivors, I hope it will provide valuable and practical information for you and other survivors everywhere. I also hope that this book will ensure that your loss will not be compounded by missed opportunities, costly mistakes and missteps.

I feel privileged to have had this opportunity to share what I have gained through my own experiences with death. My journey was bumpy at times and I felt that I would never be happy again. Fortunately, I survived my own transition and have started a very exciting new chapter in my life.

My heart goes out to you in this dark chapter of your life, but I want my message to you to be one of great hope. This too shall pass and you can find happiness despite this monumental loss.

May you also channel the energy of your loved one's life into your own wonder-filled blessing for a life-affirming and loving future.

I'd love to hear from you. Please feel free to let me know if this information was helpful to you and how I may improve it.

U.S. Mail:
Mark Colgan
179 Sully's Trail, Suite 301
Pittsford, NY 14534

E-mail: mcolgan@planyourlegacy.com

Phone: (585) 419-2272

Web: Visit our website www.planyourlegacy.com for more information.

Proceeds from this book

In honor of my late wife Joanne, I am donating a portion of the profits from this book to the Children's Heart Center at Strong Memorial Hospital in Rochester, New York. Proceeds will go to further research in the treatment of congenital heart disease and other related medical conditions in children. If you want to learn more about their programs and services to children or need more information about how to make a direct contribution to the Center, please contact me.

How to Use This Book

As a Certified Financial Planner™ professional, I was inspired to develop this handbook as a result of my own loss and the overwhelming mountain of administrative responsibilities that came with my wife's death. I also realized that while grieving, anyone—even a trained professional like myself—would have a hard time concentrating. It is critical that at this time you don't feel the need to jump into handling difficult financial matters alone, without the kind of useful information and specific directions this book or professionals can provide.

Whether you are a surviving spouse, a child, another family member or friend, *The Survivor Assistance Handbook* provides you with valuable information to guide you through the financial and administrative process following a loved one's death. In particular, this book addresses the financial and legal issues that occur within the first six to 12 months after death. To help you focus on the important issues at the appropriate time, I've organized and titled the chapters of this book to depict that timeline.

To be sure, there is no substitute for professional advice in these matters. The following pages, and especially the checklists and worksheets, give you a quick and easy way to educate and organize yourself during this period of transition. I've also added a glossary to help you understand the technical conversations that you may have with attorneys, accountants and government agencies.

Throughout this book, I also make references to many different websites that will prove valuable to you as you obtain more specific information about insurance, benefits and preventing identity theft. All of these sites are listed on the Additional Resources page at the back of the book.

This is no time to procrastinate. Despite the pain, the grief and even the numbness you might feel right now, you are a survivor. Turn the page to start taking charge of your life. Once the nitty, gritty details of your loved one's death are under control, you can begin to heal and rebuild your own life.

Chapter 1

Immediate Concerns: The Hours and Days Following Death

Even while the news of this death is still fresh in your mind, you will immediately be called upon to contact funeral homes, financial advisors, insurance agents, attorneys and family members. You will also be called upon to start making important decisions. Perhaps you are one of the lucky ones who has had a loved one willing to detail not only important information about their financial and benefits history, but also about how they would want to celebrate their life, including funeral arrangements, interment, memorial services and charitable contributions. If not, you may not know where to start.

In addition to being faced by a mountain of paperwork, new terminology and important decisions that may affect generations of your family, you are still struggling with grief. In fact, your grief may include an overwhelming amount of emotions, which can make it difficult to concentrate on and digest information about money, property and other details that are not the first things on your mind and in your heart.

If you feel this way, you are not alone. If there's one thing that is close to universally true, it is that grieving people have a hard time concentrating. No matter how smart or intellectual you may be, the emotions of grief dominate, and make focusing on mundane tasks seem impossible. For example, the reason I originally wrote *The Survivor Assistance Handbook* is because, even though I was a Certified Financial Planner professional and good old number-cruncher, I discovered that my emotions left little room to handle all of the financial, legal and administrative tasks that sprung up in the aftermath of Joanne's death.

Widows and widowers make massive errors in judgment because their brains are not firing on all cylinders. With that in mind, we strongly suggest that in any of your meetings with bankers, financial advisors, lawyers and other trusted advisors, that you bring along a trusted friend or relative—one you have empowered to listen and to ask questions on your behalf.

In the Hours Following:

■ Notify Important People and Institutions

Assign someone to contact the following people and professionals:

1. Relatives
2. Close friends
3. Clergy

4. Business associates
5. Attorney
6. Executor/Executrix
7. Financial advisor
8. Accountant
9. Funeral director
10. Organ bank/hospital (an organ donor card, below, is often carried in a wallet or purse or is indicated on the person's driver's license)
11. Employer
12. Insurance agent

■ Check Organ Donation Wishes

You may want to check the deceased's driver's license or look for an organ donor card. Here is an example of what one looks like.

Donor Card	This is a legal document under the Uniform Anatomical Gift Act or similar laws, signed by the donor and the following two witnesses in the presence of each other:
Name: _____ In the hope that I may help others, I hereby make this gift for purpose of transplant, medical study or education, to take effect upon my death. I give: ❑ Any needed organs/tissues ❑ Only the following organs/tissues _____ Limitations or special wishes, if any AMERICAN SHARE FOUNDATION, DEMPSEY AVE., VAN NUYS, CA	_____ Signature of donor Date Signed: _____ Donor's DOB: _____ _____ Signature, witness #1 _____ Signature, witness #2

■ Protect Against Burglary

Due to the public knowledge of your absence, there is a risk of break-ins during the funeral and visitation period. Thieves will also review social networking sites such as Facebook. It is best to have someone remain in the home, if possible. If there are items of significant value in the home, consider notifying your local police department of your absence, particularly if the funeral is taking place in another city. You might also consider putting your valuables in a safe deposit box or storing them at a friend's house.

■ Check for Any Pre-arrangements for Funeral and/or Burial

While a funeral director will take care of most funeral and burial arrangements, you'll want to check for any possible pre-arranged, written funeral or burial instructions. These wishes may be kept with the will, in a safety deposit box or be on file with an attorney or local funeral home. In some cases, the funeral arrangements may also have been pre-paid.

■ Be Prepared to Pay

Most funeral homes and cemeteries require their expenses to be paid prior to the service. Some will accept a life insurance assignment, but they may charge an added fee for doing so.

■ Take Advantage of Veteran's Benefits

Veterans, military service members and their dependents can be buried in a national cemetery for free or possibly receive an allowance toward funeral and burial expenses. Other benefits may include obtaining a free ceremonial American flag, a headstone and/or presidential memorial certificate. For more details, you may inquire with the National Cemetery Administration.

■ Obtain Death Certificates

Have the funeral director provide you with the proper number of death certificates. They will help you determine how many are needed. These will be used as proof of death for administering the estate, collecting life insurance, changing bank accounts, transferring titles and deeds, obtaining discounted "bereavement airfare" for relatives flying into town for the funeral, etc. Make sure to carefully check the information for accuracy and store the certificates in a secure location. Also, be aware that some states charge as much as $40 per death certificate.

■ Airline Bereavement Fares

Be aware that airline bereavement fares vary from airline to airline, but have been eliminated in most cases (or are more expensive than going online).

■ If Burial is Chosen:

- **Check to see if decedent already owns a burial plot**
  If a burial plot has been purchased in advance, a burial plot deed will have been issued to your loved one. Contact the funeral director or

designated cemetery to determine whether a copy of the burial plot deed will be required to bury the decedent. Deeds may often be stored in a safe deposit box at your bank or other secure location.

- **Contact the designated or desired cemetery**
  If a plot has not yet been acquired, consider buying two, side-by-side plots at this time for you and your spouse. You may also want to buy plots for each member of your family. Too often, people wait to do this and by the time they get back to the cemetery, the adjoining plots have been sold. Also, you might get better pricing if you buy the property in advance of need or are buying multiple plots at one time.

■ If Cremation is Chosen:

Cremation is chosen much more often than just a few years ago, and will continue to be a viable option.

- **Arrange for cremation**
  Cremation arrangements may be made through a funeral director. You will be asked to select an urn (a container for the ashes) at the same time.

- **Cremation still allows for traditional services**
  If you choose cremation, do not overlook the fact that traditional services—including viewing and visitation with the casket present—are still possible.

- **Decide what to do with the ashes**

  Later, you may choose to have the ashes scattered, buried in a gravesite, placed in an urn or some combination of these options. The ashes can also be placed in an urn and kept in a personal or private location. Or you may desire to have them stored in an above-ground niche at the cemetery or even buried in a cemetery plot. In some cases, more than one urn could be buried in a single cemetery plot, so you might start thinking about what you'd like to do for yourself.

  Whatever you choose, keep in mind that the ashes can be separated to fulfill more than one desire. For instance, you may wish to scatter half of the remains and divide the remaining half into urns for each of the family members. If the ashes are to be scattered, consider two things. First, it is illegal in many states to scatter ashes. Secondly, keep in mind that if all of the ashes are scattered, you leave behind no permanent record of your loved one's life for future generations. This could make it difficult for those friends and family who may need or wish to visit a more tangible memorial.

  Before making any irreversible decisions, discuss the options with close family and friends. If no conclusive decision arises, consider tabling such important decisions until later.

■ Go Ahead and Use the Decedent's Car

In some states, the immediate family of the deceased may continue to use the car until the deceased's registration and/or insurance expires. Contact your local department of motor vehicles to verify this.

■ Retain Transportation Receipts

Transportation expenses for immediate family members are considered to be part of the funeral expenses and are deductible, should an estate tax return be filed.

■ Keep Track of Visitors, Gifts, Donations, Flowers and Cards Received

The days immediately following the death will be filled with a flurry of activity and a parade of well-wishers. It may be difficult to respond at the time to any items that are received. Ask a friend or family member to help you keep track. Knowing who sent what will help you later when you do have the time and desire to respond to these acts of kindness. On the next page, you will find a simple worksheet. In addition to your own list, don't forget to keep a guest book at the wake and funeral so you retain a record of who came to pay their respects. You may find yourself referring to this information for many years to come.

Name	Gift	Thank You Sent?

■ Arrange to Meet with an Attorney

You may already have an attorney to work with in processing the will and estate. If not, this is the time to find legal representation. Choosing the right attorney is critical. Many lawyers, especially the good ones, don't do a lot of marketing; they attract clients by word-of-mouth. To find these attorneys, you'll have to tap into their network of clients and colleagues. You might, therefore, consider the following search methods:

1. **Ask other professionals** — Ask the attorneys and accountants you work with to recommend an estate attorney they know and trust.

2. **Ask clients** — Satisfied clients can be a good source of referrals—but exercise caution. Clients are not always the best judge of a professional's quality of work, especially in complex legal matters. You don't want a bad lawyer with a charming personality.

3. **Search legal directories** — You can search an online version of the Martindale-Hubbell directory by legal specialty and geographic location. If you don't have Internet access, check at your local library. For more details, you may also visit www.planyourlegacy.com.

4. **Call your local bar association** — Go to the American Bar Association's website www.abanet.org and click on your state for a list

of lawyer referral sources. Focus on referral sources that meet ABA standards. This means that they operate solely in the public interest and do not charge for referrals.

5. **Check for area of specialization** — Martindale-Hubbell, the company that publishes a directory of attorneys in the United States, identifies four specialties related to financial planning:

- **Trusts and estates** — includes estate planning and preparation of wills, trusts and other planning documents.
- **Wills and probate** — Most attorneys do one or both of these. Transactional lawyers handle the administrative side of probate, while probate litigators represent clients in estate claims.
- **Eldercare** — This rapidly growing area of law specializes in the needs of older people.
- **Family law** — These attorneys handle divorces and all matters relating to children, including: adoption, guardianship, child custody and child support. They also do prenuptial agreements.

6. **Lastly, consider the attorney's fees** — Some attorneys may charge by the hour; others charge a percentage of the value of the estate. In some cases, a paralegal may do much of the paperwork and will have a

different billing rate. You should inquire about the division of labor and the related costs.

■ Arrange to Meet with Your Accountant

It is important that the survivor also spend some time with the accountant. There may be tax returns due, estimated taxes to pay or other items that need to be taken care of as the pendency of the estate continues. You may even want to consider a joint meeting with the attorney and accountant. It can be well worth the expense in creating clarity; organize the things that need to be done and to get things rolling.

■ Contact the Executor/Executrix of the Estate

This person, named in the will, is the one responsible for executing the wishes of the decedent and processing the estate, including the distribution of assets to individuals and charities. The executor will work closely with the attorney and should be contacted immediately.

■ Contact the People Listed as Witnesses in the Will

Many wills executed in the last 30 years are "self-proving." This means that you don't have to locate the witnesses to prove the will is valid. If you aren't sure if the decedent's will is self-proving ask your attorney. If the will isn't self-proving, or if you anticipate a contest of the will, you will need to locate the individuals who served as witnesses and whose names and signatures appear at the end of the document.

■ File the Will and Petition

This must be done in the probate court in the county where the deceased has died, if you're seeking to be appointed executor or personal representative of the estate. If everything was jointly-owned or automatically passed to you or others by automatic beneficiary designation, there is no need to administer the estate through probate court.

The petition is a formal request to be assigned as the executor and the will proves this. Probate proves that the will is genuine and then distributes the property and other assets according to the terms of the will.

Even if you don't have to probate the will, some states require the person who has custody of the will to lodge (file) the will with the court to preserve it. This doesn't require opening a probate administration. But it will ensure that if after-discovered property which would have been subject to probate is found years after the decedent's death that the will will be available to administer that property.

■ Acquire the Contents of the Decedent's Safe Deposit Box

If you had a safety deposit box in joint name with

your loved one, you may open and empty the contents of the safe deposit box. Once at the bank, an officer will accompany you into the vault, point out the location of the box and insert one of the two keys needed to open the box. You will need to bring the other key which was given to the box owner. You should decide whether to continue the box rental or terminate it at this time. If the box was in the decedent's name alone, you will need a death certificate and certificate of appointment from surrogate's court to gain access.

■ Consider Postponing Major Financial Decisions

Recovering from a loved one's death is a dual process. In addition to the emotional toll, you also face financial issues that may have a big impact on your lifestyle. While taking control of your finances is an important step in rebuilding your life, don't rush into anything.

Most financial advisors recommend that you not make any major changes or long-term decisions about finances for at least six months to one year after your loved one's death. Perhaps the most common of these major financial decisions is whether or not to sell your home. Such permanent decisions like this one are better made after a period of time has gone by, when you will be thinking more logically rather than emotionally.

■ Maintain Cash Reserves

Cash flow should be your foremost concern at this time since it will have a direct impact on your lifestyle. Set aside sufficient cash for ongoing living expenses, especially those new or one-time expenses that will likely need to be satisfied during this extended decision-making period, including attorney's fees and possible estate taxes. There may also be some surprises along the way, so save a bit more than you think you will need, just in case.

■ Make a Detailed Budget

Make a detailed list of your income and expenses. For the first year or so, revisit it every three months to adjust either the budget or your living style appropriately. If your income has been reduced, you will need to reduce expenses.

■ Make Time to Grieve and Celebrate

While all of the above immediate concerns should be addressed, it is also imperative that you make time to grieve and celebrate the life you had with your loved one. Whether it is viewing old pictures, writing in a journal, surrounding yourself with family or writing a poem—listen to your heart and embrace the rituals you deem appropriate.

Below is a poem that I created the night Joanne died. It was my way of communicating my gratitude and love. Perhaps you too may find comfort in this poem or in one you write yourself.

MY DEAR JOANNE

I pray to you tonight with love,
our hearts still as one.
While your touch may not be near,
the company of your soul I hold dear.

Until we meet again,
let the heavens surround you with light
and all of the beautiful treasures
to which you claim right.

And as I finish my journey on Earth,
may God give me strength
and you give me hope,
for a new tomorrow I must cope.

You are the sun in my day
and the moon in my night.
You are the inspiration
that brings me life.

I love you forever.

Mark Colgan

To-Do List

____ Notify important people and professionals.

____ Protect against burglary.

____ Check for any pre-arrangements for funeral and/or burial.

____ Take advantage of veteran's benefits.

____ Obtain death certificates.

____ Contact the cemetery or arrange for cremation.

____ Keep track of visitors, gifts, donations and cards received.

____ Retain transportation receipts.

____ Arrange to meet with an attorney.

____ Arrange to meet with an accountant.

____ Contact the executor/executrix of the estate.

____ Contact the witnesses listed in the will.

____ Find the will and petition the probate court.

____ Acquire the contents of the decedent's safe deposit box.

____ Consider postponing any major financial decisions.

____ Maintain adequate cash reserves.

____ Make a detailed monthly budget.

____ _____

____ _____

____ _____

Notes

Chapter 2

Collecting
Survivor Benefits

The goal of this chapter is to help you determine whether or not you are entitled to certain survivor benefits and, if so, how to apply for them. It might be difficult to address such matters at this time; but it is critical because you will not receive any money or protection until you file the necessary forms.

■ Arrange for Distribution of Social Security Benefits

Social Security benefits are paid to survivors, children of survivors and other family members. If you qualify, you should file a benefits claim by contacting the nearest Social Security office as soon as possible. While the funeral director usually notifies the Social Security Administration, that notification is not a formal claim for benefits.

Look on the Internet or in your telephone book under U.S. Department of Health and Human Services. For more information, call the Social

Security Administration at 800-772-1213. This number will provide you with automated telephone services to get recorded information and conduct some business 24 hours a day. If you cannot handle your business through their automated services, you can speak to a Social Security representative between 7 a.m. and 7 p.m. Monday through Friday. People who are deaf or hearing-impaired may call their toll-free TTY number at 800-325-0778 also between 7 a.m. and 7 p.m. Monday through Friday.

When applying for Social Security benefits, you will need the birth and death certificate of the decedent, a marriage certificate, the birth certificates of any dependent children, Social Security numbers and copies of the decedent's most recent federal income tax return.

There are two possible benefits available for eligible survivors—a $255 lump sum death payment and a monthly survivor benefit. To collect either of these benefits, you must be an eligible survivor and the decedent must have been either currently insured or fully insured. To collect widow(er)'s or child's benefits, you do not have to meet the work requirement yourself. Instead, you must be the wife, widow or child of a worker who meets the requirement.

■ Determining if Decedent was Currently or Fully Insured

To be currently insured, the decedent worker must have earned at least six quarters of coverage during the 13 calendar quarter periods ending with the quarter of their death. The calendar quarters are as follows: first quarter - January, February, March; second quarter - April, May, June; third quarter - July, August, September; fourth quarter - October, November, December.

As complicated as this may sound, figuring it out is easy if you just take the quarter and year of death and subtract three from the year. Then, determine the quarter of the resulting year which corresponds to the quarter of death. This is when the period began. For example, Pat died on May 15, 2009. This is in the second quarter of 2009. We subtract three from 2009, which equals 2006. The 13-quarter period begins with the second quarter of 2006 and ends with the second quarter of 2009. If Pat earned six quarters of coverage during that period, including the beginning and ending quarters, he is currently insured.

If the deceased had achieved the "current insured" status, then they have satisfied the requirement for benefits such as Surviving Child's Benefits, Mother's/Father's Benefits—also called Young Widow(er)'s Benefits—and the Lump Sum Death Benefit.

To be fully insured for survivor benefits, the decedent worker must have earned one quarter of coverage for every year after the year of attainment of age 22 up to and including the year they died. The minimum number of quarters of coverage required in any case is six. The maximum is 40. Note that Social Security rules provide that you attain your age on the day before your birthday. If your birthday is on January 1, you attain age 22 in the year before that birthday for purposes of figuring the insured status requirement.

Here are some examples:

Quarters Required for Survivor Benefits for People Born in 1930 or Later

Age at DOD	Minimum Number of Quarters of Coverage Required
28 and younger	6
30	8
40	18
50	28
60	38
62 and older	40

It is also important to know that the insured status requirement does not affect the amount of the benefit. It is simply a minimum work requirement which must be met before any benefit is payable. Once this minimum is met, a benefit amount is computed based on average earnings.

Also, don't forget that to collect widow(er)'s or child's benefits you do not have to meet the work requirement yourself. Instead, you must be the widow, widower or child of a worker who met the requirement.

■ Who Gets Which Benefits

Once you have determined the decedent's insured status, you can evaluate which benefits are due and who is eligible to collect them. If the decedent is currently or fully insured, a $255 lump sum is payable to the widow/widower who was living with the decedent at the time of death.

Regardless of whether or not there was joint residency, this lump sum may still be collected if the widow/widower or children are immediately eligible for monthly benefits.

Determining who qualifies for monthly survivor benefits is a bit more complex. Essentially, you may collect benefits if you are a qualifying widow/widower, the deceased's minor or disabled child or a dependent parent.

To be a <u>qualifying widow/widower</u>, you must have been married to the decedent for at least nine months before their death (unless death is due to an accident or military duty) or be a divorced spouse whose marriage lasted at least ten years or be the parent of deceased's child (natural or adopted). Additionally, you must be 60 years or older, or if disabled, you must be 50 to 59 years of age, or caring for the deceased's child who is under age 16 or disabled and currently receiving Social Security benefits.

There is one exception. In general, a widow/widower cannot receive benefits if he or she remarries before age of 60 (50, if disabled) unless the subsequent marriage ends by death, divorce or annulment. However, remarriage after age 60 (50, if disabled) will not prevent payments on a former spouse's record.

To qualify as the _deceased's minor or disabled child_, you must be either a natural child, adopted child or stepchild who was at least 50 percent dependent on the deceased for support, or be a dependent grandchild in the event that your parents are deceased or disabled. Additionally, you must be unmarried and under age 18 (up to 19, if still in high school) or any age if your disability occurred before the age of 22.

Lastly, if you were a _dependent parent_ age 62 or older, you may collect monthly survivor benefits if, at the time of your child's death, you were receiving 50 percent of your support from the deceased.

If the decedent was properly insured and you qualify to begin collecting monthly survivor benefits, the amount of your benefit is based on the average lifetime earnings of the deceased. The more he or she has paid into Social Security, the higher the benefits will be. The amount a survivor receives is a percentage of the deceased's basic Social Security benefit. The table below provides examples of the most typical situations:

Classification	Benefits
Widow/widower full retirement age or older	100%
Widow/widower age 60 to full retirement age	about 71.5% to 99%
Disabled widow/widower age 50 to 59	71.5%
Widow/widower caring for a child under 16	75%
A child under age 18 (up to 19 if in high school)	75%

Percentages for a surviving divorced spouse would be the same as above.

For more information, call 1-800-772-1213 and ask for Publication No. 05-10084: *Social Security Survivor Benefits* or you can access it at www.ssa.gov.

■ Starting the Social Security Claims Process

When you are ready to begin the process, whether it's by phone or in person, make your contact as smooth as possible. Don't delay filing your claim just because you don't have all the documents. Be ready to answer the following questions and have as many of the required documents as possible.

- Your name and Social Security number
- Your name at birth (if different)

- The deceased's name, gender, date of birth and Social Security number
- Your date of birth and place of birth (U. S. state or foreign country)
- Your deceased child's date and place of death
- Whether a public or religious record was made of your birth before age 5
- Your citizenship status
- Whether you have used any other Social Security number
- The state or foreign country of the worker's fixed permanent residence at the time of death
- Whether you or anyone else has ever filed for Social Security benefits, Medicare or Supplemental Security Income on your behalf (if so, they will also ask for information on whose Social Security record you applied)
- Whether the deceased ever filed for Social Security benefits, Medicare or Supplemental Security Income (if so, they will also ask for information on whose Social Security record they applied)
- Whether you became unable to work because of illness or injury at any time within the past 14 months (if "Yes," they will also ask you the date you became unable to work)
- Whether the deceased was unable to work because of illness or injury at any time during the 14 months before their death (if "Yes," they

will also ask you the date they were unable to work)

- Whether you or the deceased was in active military service before 1968 and, if so, the dates of service and whether you have received or are eligible to receive a pension from a military or federal civilian agency
- Whether you or the deceased worked for the railroad industry
- Whether you or the deceased ever earned Social Security credits under another country's Social Security system
- Whether you qualify for or expect to receive a pension or annuity based on your own employment with the federal government of the United States or one of its states or local subdivisions
- The names, dates of birth (or age) and Social Security numbers (if known) of any of your or the deceased's former spouses
- The dates of each of your marriages and, for marriages that have ended, how and when they ended
- The dates of each of the deceased's marriages and how and when they ended
- The amount of the deceased's earnings in the year of his or her death and the preceding year
- Whether the deceased had earnings in all years since 1978
- Your earnings for this year, last year and estimated for next year

- Whether the deceased had a parent who was dependent on the deceased for half of their support at the time of their death or at the time the deceased became disabled
- Whether you were living with the deceased at the time of their death
- Whether you have any unsatisfied felony warrants for your arrest or unsatisfied federal or state warrants for your arrest for any violations of the conditions of your parole or probation
- The month you want your benefits to begin

■ Other Government Benefits

If the deceased was employed by the government and you are a potential beneficiary, be sure to check into whether or not you may qualify for Federal Employee's Retirement System (FERS) benefits, Civil Service Retirement System (CSRS) benefits, state government benefits, military personnel benefits, etc. These benefits may provide death payments, burial expenses, pension income, health benefits, education assistance, loans and more.

This is a lot of information, but gathering it in advance will save you time and frustration during the interview.

■ Beginning the Life Insurance Claims Process

Although it may seem a bit awkward to collect life insurance from the death of your loved one, it is a necessary action. Life insurance often provides you with your single biggest financial benefit. Depending on the benefit amount, it may determine whether you have to sell your home, go back to work or can count on financial security.

The sources below and on the next page can provide you with information about any life insurance benefits:

- Decedent's recent and previous employers
- Your employer for any spousal life insurance
- Lenders for mortgages, personal loans or credit cards
- Many social organizations, professional associations and unions may also offer group life insurance plans for members that provide special benefits for surviving spouses. For example, if the deceased was a member of a teacher's union, it may be possible that they owned a group life insurance policy

After this discovery process, carefully evaluate the different ways you can receive your benefits:

- **Lump sum** — the entire death benefit in one check
- **Specific income provision** — the life insurance company will pay principal and interest on a predetermined schedule
- **Life income option** — you are guaranteed income for the duration of your life. The income amount

will depend on the policy's death benefit and
your age

- **Interest income option**–the life insurance
company will hold the proceeds of the policy and
pay the interest earned. If you choose this option,
the policy's death benefit will remain intact and
be paid to your children or a secondary
beneficiary upon your death

Lastly, take the time now to review/update the
beneficiaries named on your life insurance
policies (and IRAs), especially if the deceased was
one of your beneficiaries

■ Next Steps in the Insurance Claim Process

For group policies, follow the instructions given to
you by the governing organization. For personally-
owned life insurance, contact the company whose
name and address appears on the policy, your
insurance agent or call the company's local office. If
the decedent owned life insurance, but the policy
cannot be located or the agent's name is lost, contact
the American Council of Life Insurers (Policy Search,
ACLI) 1001 Pennsylvania Avenue, N.W., Washington
D.C. 20003 or online www.acli.com. They will search
all recorded policies for free and provide information
you need to process your claim.

If you are listed as the beneficiary on the policy, order a claim form and prepare a claim package. Normally, your agent will help you do this; however, if you do not have an agent, we've provided you with a sample letter that you can use to start the process.

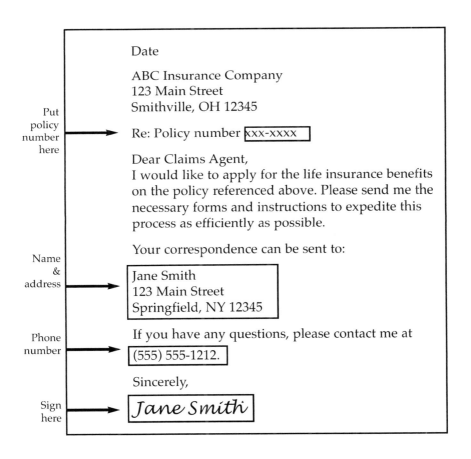

Put policy number here →

Name & address →

Phone number →

Sign here →

Date

ABC Insurance Company
123 Main Street
Smithville, OH 12345

Re: Policy number xxx-xxxx

Dear Claims Agent,
I would like to apply for the life insurance benefits on the policy referenced above. Please send me the necessary forms and instructions to expedite this process as efficiently as possible.

Your correspondence can be sent to:

Jane Smith
123 Main Street
Springfield, NY 12345

If you have any questions, please contact me at (555) 555-1212.

Sincerely,

Jane Smith

When you receive the paperwork, you may need:
- A certified copy of the death certificate
- The insurance policy number
- The amount listed as the death benefit or face value
- The decedent's occupation and last day of work
- The decedent's birth certificate (or other birth documentation) and your own birth certificate, depending on how you want the proceeds to be paid

Insurance companies may also request information about the circumstances of the decedent's death, including:
- Attending physician's statement
- Coroner's report
- Police incident report
- The beneficiary's age, address and Social Security number for federal government filings

However, remember that life insurance proceeds are generally not considered to be taxable income to the beneficiary. In some cases, the insurance proceeds could be taxed for estate tax purposes. There are also some other conditions where life insurance could be taxed, for example, life insurance within an IRA or pension plan or a policy that had some kind of transfer for value transaction. In addition, some wills provide that any share of estate tax related to insurance proceeds should be paid from those proceeds. The bottom line is that you should check with a qualified accountant to determine your exact situation.

Regardless of your situation, request IRS Form 712 from the insurance company at the same time the claim for the proceeds is filed. You may need it depending upon the circumstances under which your estate must file an estate tax return. Ask your attorney for more information.

■ Collecting Employee Benefits

Contact current and all former employers of the decedent to collect the full amount of all employee benefits due to you. This is one step that many people often forget to follow through on, but you may be eligible to receive:

- The decedent's unpaid salary
- Accrued vacation and sick pay
- Workers' compensation benefits

■ Determining Retirement Benefits

A beneficiary can fall into one of the following categories: spouse, non-spouse or entity, such as a trust. Depending upon what type of beneficiary you are, the I.R.S. will often dictate your options. Be sure to talk with a financial consultant and review your options thoroughly.

Furthermore, beneficiaries need to know that, at a certain point, they will have to start taking Required Minimum Distributions (RMD) from inherited IRAs. The intent of these rules is to prevent families from handing down IRA monies from generation to generation and deferring taxes forever. Once an IRA owner dies, the beneficiary rules kick in—and it's only a matter of time before mandatory distributions must begin.

To better understand your distribution options for IRA accounts, please refer to Chapter 7.

■ Assessing Employer Health Insurance

One of the biggest financial worries you may have is how to maintain your health insurance. If you are a widow or widower, you are eligible for health coverage through COBRA (Consolidated Omnibus Budget Reconciliation Act of 1985). COBRA covers the deceased's enrolled eligible family members for up to 36 months (more than the standard COBRA 18-month period) after the spouse's death—as long as your spouse was employed at the time of death and was covered by the company's health insurance plan. Survivors must still pay the premiums for the plan, but you will not have to find, qualify for or pay for a new health insurance plan right away.

Under COBRA, you will be required to pay the full cost of the insurance plus a two percent administrative fee. In cases where the employer was paying a good portion of the monthly premium, the rate you may have to pay under COBRA will likely change.

For COBRA appeals information or notification rights, you should contact the U.S. Department of Labor Pension and Welfare Benefits Administration Division of Technical Assistance and Inquiries, 200 Constitution Ave., NW (Room N-5658), Washington, D.C. 20210 or call (202) 219-8784 or (202) 219-8776.

Competitive medical insurance quotes can be obtained online at www.ehealthinsurance.com.

■ Taking Advantage of Flex Benefits

Also, make sure to ask the decedent's employer if there was a medical flexible spending (flex) or reimbursement account for the deceased. A flex account allows for the reimbursement of out-of-pocket health expenses (those not covered by health insurance) from pre-tax dollars deducted from an employee's paycheck. Therefore, an employee's taxable income will be reduced by the amount placed in the account. If so, make sure you file a claim for any outstanding medical bills incurred by the deceased before the end of the calendar year or this money will be lost.

Flexible spending accounts are "use-it-or-lose-it" plans. This means that amounts in the account at the end of the plan year cannot be carried over to the next year. In some cases, the plan may provide a grace period of up to $2^1/_2$ months after the end of the plan year. If so, any qualified medical expenses incurred in that period are treated as having occurred in the previous plan year and can be paid from any amounts left in the account at the end of that year. Any monies not properly withdrawn are completely lost as your employer is not permitted to refund any part of the balance to you.

■ Collecting Veteran's Benefits

The Department of Veterans Affairs (VA) offers certain benefits and services to honor deceased veterans. The benefits include reimbursement of up to $2,000 of burial expenses, a headstone or marker, burial flag, burial in a VA National Cemetery and, for eligible recipients, a Presidential Memorial Certificate. If you forgot to collect these benefits, you should know that there is no time limit on claims for reimbursement of burial expenses for a service-related death. In other cases, claims must be filed within two years of the veteran's burial.

Benefits may also be available for dependents and survivors. A death pension is payable to some surviving spouses and children of deceased wartime veterans.

Additionally, the VA Civilian Health and Medical Program (CHAMPVA) shares the cost of medical services for eligible dependents and survivors of certain veterans. There are no time limits for these benefits.

Whether surviving family members are paid such benefits will depend on a number of factors, including whether the veteran died from causes connected with military service, whether he or she served in war or peacetime and whether the discharge was honorable or not. The surviving family's financial circumstances are also a consideration.

To check on any benefits you may be eligible for, call (800) 827-1000, or visit your local Veterans Administration (VA) office. If there is no local VA office, you may contact the Veterans of Foreign Wars or the American Legion, or even the American Red Cross. The VA will need a veteran's claim number (called a "C" number) or a copy of the Certificate of Discharge from military service (DD Form 214), a military service number or branch of service and dates served. In addition, a death certificate, marriage certificate(s) and birth certificates for children may be required.

To-Do List

_____ Arrange for distribution of Social Security benefits.

_____ Start the Social Security claims process.

_____ Collect life insurance proceeds.

_____ Collect employee benefits.

_____ Determine retirement benefits.

_____ Assess employer health insurance.

_____ Take advantage of flex benefits.

_____ Collect veteran's benefits.

_____ _____

_____ _____

_____ _____

_____ _____

_____ _____

_____ _____

_____ _____

_____ _____

_____ _____

_____ _____

_____ _____

_____ _____

_____ _____

Notes

Chapter 3

Getting Organized and Sorting Through the Paperwork

Remembering to take time to grieve is important and many things can wait! Being organized prevents you from missing deadlines or misplacing important documents amidst the upheaval that typically accompanies the loss of a loved one. Survivors often become overwhelmed with the mountain of paperwork from insurance and mortgage companies, creditors and banks, the decedent's employer and many other businesses and individuals. Such correspondence can mount up quickly.

The First Step

Resist any temptation to initially throw away any relevant correspondence as a way of simplifying your life. Initially, it may be difficult to decide what is important and what is not. With time, you will gain a better grasp of what is important and what can be discarded.

A relatively simple way to organize all the mail, documentation and paperwork is to start a filing system. Whether you use folders or large manila envelopes in a filing cabinet or just piles on the dining room table, the point is to retain these documents in a secure place and create a system for easy retrieval.

Consider using folders or piles for each type of correspondence. Use Post-It® Notes or other clear markings to indicate due dates in plain view. In short, pick a system that works for you.

Below and on the next few pages, you will find a list of suggested categories and documents for each folder or pile. While this system may take some time to set up, it will provide an efficient way to retain and retrieve important documents.

Estate Documents

Wills, codicils, supporting memoranda
Trust agreements
Powers of Attorney
Powers of Appointment

Life Insurance

Life insurance policies
Copy of claim forms
IRS Form 712 (to report life insurance proceeds)

Correspondence from Employer

Benefit claim forms
Paycheck stubs
Benefit plan statements

Tax Information

Copies of individual tax returns for the past three years
Receipts for other taxes paid
Charitable contribution receipts
Other deductible items

Business-Related

Partnership agreements
Joint venture agreements
Contracts

Correspondence from Banks

Savings account statements and passbook
Checking account statements, register and canceled checks

Household

Property deed
Homeowner's insurance policy
Appraisals
Records and receipts for home improvements

Bills

List of bills — paid and unpaid

Credit Card Statements

Automobile Papers

Title and registration
Automobile insurance policy

Decedent's Personal Documentation

Death certificates

Birth certificate

Social Security card

Military papers

Family's Documentation

Birth certificates

Social Security numbers

Marriage certificates

Divorce agreements

Honorable/dishonorable discharge certificates

Investment Information

Brokerage account statements

Money market accounts

Certificates of deposit

Stock and bond certificates

Mutual funds - IRAs

U.S. Savings bonds

U.S. Treasury securities

List of All Other Assets Owned by Decedent

Real estate

Stocks and Bonds

Mutual Funds

Savings accounts

Certificate of deposits

Personal property

To-Do List

____ Retain all relevant correspondence.

____ Buy folders or large manila envelopes.

____ Collect life insurance policies and claims forms.

____ Collect estate-related documents.

____ Collect employer benefits paperwork and claims forms.

____ Find last three years of tax returns and receipts.

____ Collect business-related agreements and contracts.

____ Assemble bank statements, canceled checks and register.

____ Put together house-related papers.

____ Collect paid and unpaid bills and credit card statements.

____ Locate automobile title, registration and insurance policy.

____ Locate decedent's personal documentation—birth and death certificates, Social Security card and military papers.

____ Collect personal documentation from your family.

____ Locate investment and other asset documentation.

____ _____

____ _____

____ _____

Notes

Chapter 4

Reviewing Assets

Prior to paying any bills or distributing any monies, it is a good idea to review all of your assets. This will give you a better understanding of what you have to work with and what needs to be addressed.

On the surface, your savings and investments may seem straightforward. However, there may be some complications that are not obvious. For example, you might own bonds with maturity dates, CD's with estate clauses, investment partnerships with cash call provisions and so on. If you own rental property, it might have created cash flow over the years, but if the decedent did not take care of the property properly, you might be facing significant deferred maintenance. As you can see, it is important to marshal all of the assets but it is also equally important to get a basic understanding of what they are, the rights and obligations related to the ownership of them and if they represent a net cash inflow or outflow.

So, given the above possible complications and the possibility that your attorney may have implemented post-mortem planning techniques, make sure to seek the advice of an attorney prior to exercising any of these action items.

■ Evaluating Accounts and Existing Bank Relationships

Get a handle on all of the existing checking, savings, money market or Certificate of Deposit (CD) accounts, held individually or jointly in the decedent's name.

With your attorney's approval, discuss with representatives of each bank the possibility of switching joint accounts to an individual account in your name. If you are not sure which banks must be contacted, check the previous year's tax return. If a Schedule B was filed with the tax return, you may be able to obtain information about the pertinent institutions as they are often listed in the section titled Interest Income.

■ Evaluating Options for Retirement Accounts

If your loved one had an Individual Retirement Account (IRA) and you are named as the beneficiary, be sure to carefully explore all of your distribution options. This topic is thoroughly discussed in Chapter 7.

■ Transferring Stocks, Bonds and Brokerage Accounts

If your attorney authorizes it, contact the brokers at each firm to have them transfer jointly-owned securities to you or the surviving owner(s). They may require resending copies of the death certificate before the transfer can be made.

In some cases, you may have stocks held outside of your brokerage firm. Some people prefer to hold stock certificates on their own rather than with their broker. Should this be the case, you will need to contact the transfer agent listed on the stock's corresponding statement.

If you aren't sure whether or not you have securities held outside your brokerage account, make a list of all the companies from which you are receiving dividend checks and compare them to the list of securities held in your brokerage account. If you discover that you are in fact receiving checks from additional companies, contact each company's investor relations department.

■ Check on Current Mortgages and Notes Receivable

Check to see if the decedent held any mortgages on residential or commercial property or held notes on automobiles or other personal property which had been sold to individuals or businesses. There may also be outstanding personal loans for which payments are due. All of these assets are considered part of the estate. Make sure that the monthly payments are directed to the appropriate person or persons as determined by the will or executor of the estate.

■ Check on Title for Real Estate

If your home was held in joint name, the title does not necessarily need to be changed. The property may automatically become the property of the surviving owner. If the real estate was in the sole name of the deceased, then the title must be changed to list the beneficiaries' name(s) as the new owner(s). This would be done as part of the probate process.

■ Keep or Cash Out Annuities

Check any annuities held in the decedent's name to determine the amount of the death benefit due you or other survivors. In some instances, beneficiaries may be entitled to the policy's highest anniversary value. The easiest way to determine this is to speak with your insurance agent. Also, consult with an accountant or tax professional to consider the tax ramifications when deciding whether to keep or cash out the annuity.

■ Transferring Ownership of Automobiles, Boats and Vehicles

Remember, by law, a member of the immediate family of the deceased owner may continue to use the vehicle until the registration or insurance expires.

Eventually, when it comes time to change ownership of the vehicle you will need to establish its value—this will dictate your next step.

Refer to Chapter 8 for more information about how to go about transferring ownership of vehicles.

To-Do List

_____ Review all your assets.

_____ Evaluate existing accounts.

_____ Evaluate existing bank relationships.

_____ Transfer jointly-owned securities to beneficiaries.

_____ Locate any stock certificates held by decedent.

_____ Check on any current mortgages and notes receivable.

_____ Locate the title for all real estate holdings.

_____ Evaluate whether to keep or cash out annuities.

_____ Transfer ownership of cars, boats and other vehicles.

_____ _____

_____ _____

_____ _____

_____ _____

_____ _____

_____ _____

_____ _____

_____ _____

_____ _____

_____ _____

Notes

Chapter 5

Paying the Bills

For many of us, mounting bills will be cause for some anxiety, but there are definite rules for how and when to pay bills held in the sole name of the decedent. This chapter will help you sort through the pile, pay appropriate bills and conserve the assets of the estate.

First, don't be in a rush to pay off the decedent's bills. And although you might feel like you're being helpful, absolutely don't pay off the decedent's debts from your own funds.

The estate is responsible for satisfying debts of the decedent and the available funds should go first to pay for funeral expenses, then attorneys and lastly creditors. In other words, if the estate runs out of money before the creditors (including hospitals) get paid, you may not have to pay them. Bottom line: consult with your attorney before paying any bills.

■ First, Pay Funeral Expenses

Funeral expenses may be deductible from the decedent's federal estate tax return, so care must also be taken to gather proof of payment for all of the expenses, including those for the funeral director, burial plot, headstone or cremation.

■ Notifying Creditors and Determining Balance Due

Contact all creditors and check for insurance on outstanding loans, mortgages and credit cards. The deceased may have carried life insurance on those borrowings. If there was insurance on any of these installment loans, the entire balance due may be paid off by the policy.

■ Terminating Vehicle Leases

If you don't want to keep the decedent's vehicle, see if the lease has a death clause. If so, you may be able to get out of the lease at no cost and simply return the vehicle. Ford Credit, for example, has a program called "Peace of Mind," which allows customers who are 62 years of age or older to lease or finance a new vehicle without the worry of creating a future financial burden for their families.

Peace of Mind provides options designed to enable a family or estate to adjust in the event a customer should pass away before completing the lease or finance contract—at no extra cost. These options include the opportunity to keep the vehicle or to turn it in and be freed of the remaining contractual obligations. If you do not discover a death clause, you still may have some protection because the lease remains a liability of the estate, not the survivor, so long as you did not sign or co-sign the lease.

■ Terminating Cell Phone Contracts

If you no longer need the decedent's cell phone, see if the contract has a death or buy-out clause. If so, you may be able to terminate the contract without any further obligations or at the very least have the disconnect fee waived. If not, the contract obligation remains a liability of the estate, not the survivor, so long as you did not sign or co-sign the contract.

■ Transferring Mortgages and Notes Payable

Generally speaking, mortgages and notes payable follow the asset to which they are attached. So, whomever is awarded ownership of the decedent's property will be responsible for satisfying the corresponding mortgage or lien against it. Care must be taken to ensure that these are paid in a timely manner. Don't forget to check on any possible mortgage insurance benefits!

■ Closing Online Accounts

If the decedent had any accounts with online retailers, held any web-based subscriptions with magazines, research or virus protection service providers, you should consider either closing or updating these online accounts with the proper user and billing/shipping information.

■ Meet Charitable Pledges

It is both a contractual and an ethical obligation to "make good" on any outstanding pledges to charities. Review the decedent's checking account for the past two years and look for monies sent to charities. This will help you identify those charities that were supported through annual giving programs set up by the decedent.

■ Managing Income Taxes

A surviving spouse may file a joint tax return for the tax year in which the death occurred. However, a final joint return with the decedent cannot be filed if the surviving spouse remarried before the end of the year. The filing status of the decedent in this instance should be married filing separately.

A surviving spouse with dependent children may be eligible to use Qualifying Widow(er) with Dependent Child as the filing status for two years following the year of death of their spouse. For example, if the spouse died in 2006, and the survivor does not remarry, they may be able to use this filing status for both the 2007 and 2008 tax years as well.

This filing status entitles you to use joint return tax rates and the highest standard deduction amount if you do not itemize deductions. This status does not entitle you to file a joint return.

The surviving spouse is eligible to file their 2006 tax return as a Qualifying Widow(er) with Dependent Child if they meet all of the following tests:

- The surviving spouse was entitled to file a joint return with their spouse for the year their spouse died. It does not matter whether or not a joint return was actually filed.
- The surviving spouse did not remarry before the end of the tax year in which the decedent died.
- The spouse has a child, stepchild, adopted child or foster child for whom they can claim an exemption.
- The surviving spouse paid more than half the cost of keeping up a home that is the main home for themselves and their child for the entire year, except for temporary absences.

Example

John Reed's wife died in 2004. John has not remarried. During 2005 and 2006, he continued to keep up a home for himself and his child (for whom he can claim an exemption). For 2004, he was entitled to file a joint return for himself and his deceased wife. In 2005 and 2006, he can file as <u>qualifying widower with a dependent child.</u> After 2006, he can file as Head of Household, if he qualifies.

The IRS booklet, Publication 559 *Information for Survivors, Executors and Administrators* may be helpful. You can order a copy of this publication by going online to www.irs.gov or by calling the IRS forms distribution center at (800) 829-3676. As with all tax matters, it is best to consult with your accountant or tax professional before taking any action.

■ Paying Estate Taxes

Generally speaking, if a federal estate tax return must be filed, taxes are due within nine months of the date of death. However, there are conditions under which an estate can ask for an extension of time to pay death taxes. In those cases, where the government grants an extension, the estate will pay interest on the amount of unpaid taxes. An attorney or accountant can help you navigate through those waters. If the estate tax is not paid within nine months and an extension has not been granted, you will owe substantial interest and penalties.

As of the writing of this book, the legislation surrounding estate tax is very much up in the air. While many estates will not be taxable, it is important not to assume that any particular estate is not. Because tax laws frequently change, you will need to contact an accountant or tax attorney to understand your options and determine the most beneficial course of action.

To-Do List

____ Don't pay the decedent's bills with your own funds.

____ First, pay funeral expenses and retain receipts.

____ Consult with your attorney before paying other bills.

____ Notify creditors of the death.

____ Check to see if there was life insurance on any loans, mortgages and credit cards.

____ Terminate vehicle lease and/or see if there was a death clause on the car lease.

____ Cancel cell phone contracts.

____ Transfer mortgages and notes to new owners.

____ Close any accounts with online retailers, cancel online subscriptions, etc.

____ Meet charitable obligations.

____ Determine filing status for income tax returns.

____ File federal estate tax returns within nine months.

____ _____

____ _____

____ _____

____ _____

____ _____

____ _____

Notes

Chapter 6

Understanding IRA Distribution Options

This chapter is dedicated to the complexities of today's IRA accounts and is intended to provide you with guidelines for understanding your beneficiary status, eligibility and distribution options. For more information, go to www.irs.gov or order I.R.S. Publication 575 or better yet, seek the counsel of a Certified Financial Planner™ professional. Structuring your retirement benefits properly is critical, as it will directly affect your lifestyle.

Deciding what to do with an inherited IRA is among the most important and complex decisions you will face. After all, choosing the right strategy can significantly impact the amount of income tax the beneficiary is liable for. So, let's carefully review the options you'll want to ponder.

If you don't need all or some of these assets and you'd like a younger beneficiary to be able to maximize the potential for tax-deferred growth by stretching distributions out over their lifetime, you may wish to disclaim all or part of your IRA inheritance.

A disclaimer is an irrevocable decision to give up your right to inherit the IRA assets. If you want to take advantage of this option, you must disclaim the assets before you've actually taken possession of them and do so within nine months of the IRA owner's death.

If you choose to inherit the IRA assets, your first step is to transfer the decedent's IRA assets into an IRA Beneficiary Distribution Account (IRA-BDA). Then you must carefully review your distribution options and elect the method that best meets your needs.

Your distribution options generally depend on whether the IRA owner died before or after April 1st of the year following the year in which he or she turned age $70^{1}/_{2}$. That's when the owner would have been required to start taking minimum distributions from the account. We'll refer to that date as the "required beginning date."

Your options also vary depending on what type of beneficiary you are. Generally, a beneficiary will fall into one of the following categories: non-spouse, spouse or estate.

Let's first assume that you're not the surviving spouse of the deceased IRA owner, but this person was kind enough to name you as the beneficiary of the IRA.

■ Guidelines for the Non-Spouse Beneficiary

Options for non-spouse, if the IRA owner died <u>after</u> the required beginning distribution date include:

- **Take a Lump-Sum Distribution**
  You can elect to receive the entire balance immediately in a total distribution. However, your distribution will be taxed as ordinary income in the year the distribution is taken. So, unless you really need the money immediately, it might be better to leave it in the IRA as long as possible, defer taxation and prolong the period of tax-deferred growth.

- **Spread Out Distributions Over Longest Life**
  If the IRA owner had already begun to receive required minimum distributions, the remaining distributions must be paid out for the longer of your single life expectancy or the IRA owner's life expectancy as determined by the I.R.S. The decedent's last distribution must be taken by December 31 in the year of death. The beneficiary's first distribution must be taken by December 31 of the following year and each succeeding year.

Options for the non-spouse, if the IRA owner died <u>before</u> the required beginning distribution date:

- **Take a Lump-Sum Distribution**
  You can elect to receive the entire balance immediately. However, your distribution will be taxed as ordinary income in the year the distribution is taken. So, unless you really need the money immediately, it's generally better to leave it in the IRA as long as possible, defer taxation and prolong the period of tax-deferred growth.

- **Spread Out Distributions Over Your Life**
  If the decedent had not yet started taking required minimum distributions, these must be paid out over your single life expectancy. Please note that if you elect to take this option, it's vital that you take the initial distribution by the end of the year following the year of the IRA owner's death. If no election is made, you may be required to take distributions using the five-year rule as described below.

- **Defer Distributions Over Five Years**
  You must withdraw the entire balance by December 31 of the year which marks the fifth anniversary of the IRA owner's death. Distributions may be made at any time during the five-year period in order to spread out the income tax liability.

■ Guidelines for the Surviving Spouse

If you are the surviving spouse, you have all the same options as a non-spouse beneficiary and the additional option of treating yourself as the owner.

If you become the owner, you can avoid the post-death minimum distribution rules completely and defer any distributions until after reaching age $70^1/_2$. This choice can be advantageous if you are younger than the deceased IRA owner.

If you have not yet reached age $70^1/_2$, but your spouse had, it enables you to stretch out the tax deferral of IRA assets by delaying required minimum distributions (RMD) until you reach the age of $70^1/_2$. Taking ownership also gives you the opportunity to name another beneficiary, which means you can also stretch out tax deferral for another generation. Incidentally, naming a younger beneficiary can also reduce your required minimum distributions because you can base them on the joint life expectancy with the new beneficiary. The election to treat an inherited IRA as your own can be made by filing an election on a form supplied by the IRA trustee or custodian, by simply not taking required distributions, or by making a contribution to the IRA.

While it is nice to have the option of treating yourself as the owner, it may not always be the best choice. If you were older than your spouse, and your spouse died before the age of 70$\frac{1}{2}$, transferring the decedent's IRA assets into an IRA Beneficiary Distribution Account (IRA-BDA) would be more advantageous since this option would allow you to delay taking the required minimum distributions.

This is also an excellent option if you are younger than the age of 59$\frac{1}{2}$ and you need to supplement your income. Any distributions would receive a special exception for death and not be subject to a 10 percent federal income tax penalty.

■ Distribution Options for the Estate

If the IRA owner didn't name a person or his estate as beneficiary, there is little room for distribution planning.

If the IRA owner died on or after the required beginning date, the balance must be distributed over the IRA owner's single life expectancy, reduced by one for each year since the year of death.

On the other hand, if the IRA owner died before the required beginning date, the balance must be distributed by the end of the fifth year following the year of the owner's death.

Example

The owner died in 2005 at the age of 80. The owner's traditional IRA went to his estate. The account balance at the end of 2005 was $100,000. In 2006, the required minimum distribution was $10,870 ($100,000 ÷ 9.2). (9.2 is the owner's life expectancy at the time of death, 10.2, reduced by one year.) If the owner had died in 2005 at the age of 70, the entire account would have to be distributed by the end of 2010.

■ Distribution Guidelines for those Inheriting a Roth IRA

If a Roth IRA owner dies, the minimum distribution rules that apply to traditional IRAs also apply to Roth IRAs as though the Roth IRA owner died before his or her required beginning date.

If you are a non-spousal beneficiary, you must take distributions either by the end of the year marking the fifth anniversary of the account owner's death or over your own life expectancy, starting no later than December 31 of the year following death.

Distributions will be income tax free at the time of withdrawal as long as the original owner of the Roth IRA met the requirements for qualified distributions. Distributions would not be subject to the 10 percent early withdrawal penalty.

If you are a spousal beneficiary, you can keep the Roth IRA and delay distributions until the decedent would have reached the age of $70^1/_2$, or treat the Roth IRA as your own and avoid the post-death minimum distribution rules completely. Taking ownership would also give you the opportunity to contribute additional retirement money to the account.

■ Guidelines for Those Inheriting a Qualified Retirement Plan

If you are inheriting assets from the decedent's qualified retirement plan such as a 401k or 403b plan, the distribution options may be entirely different. Some qualified retirement plans force distributions to the beneficiaries all at once. This can present issues given the fact that the beneficiary must pay income tax on the amount received.

Make sure you review the plan distribution options with plan administrator at the decedent's place of employment. Remember to check in with past employers to see if you are eligible to receive monies from any and all funded retirement plans.

Notes

Chapter 7

Processing and Managing the Estate: The Executor's Checklist

Once you have made a decision on how to handle your IRA distributions, you have all your assets calculated and the outstanding bills are under control, finalizing the decedent's estate will undoubtedly be your next concern.

The executor, executrix or administrator is the person to carry out this responsibility. He or she will be responsible for administering and distributing the decedent's property and carrying out the wishes specified in the will. The person selected may be a spouse, child, close relative, friend or trusted professional. In cases where the decedent does not have a will, then they are said to have died intestate, and it will be up to the court to appoint an administrator(s) regardless of the size of the estate. The court-appointed administrator would have the same responsibilities as the executor/executrix.

An executor's role varies from state to state. In general, this person is charged with listing the assets of the decedent's estate, collecting monies owed to it and paying the estate's debts. Executors are also responsible for disbursing property to the appropriate beneficiaries. A decedent's will may also specifically authorize other responsibilities or powers.

While it is recommended and often common practice to hire an attorney for advice in settling the estate, it is not mandatory. If the estate is small and uncomplicated, it may be possible to handle the estate administration without hiring an attorney.

In New York, for example, estates less than $20,000 that do not contain real estate can be processed through Surrogate's Court for about $1.00.

■ Gathering All Significant Documents

The person managing the decedent's affairs bears the ultimate responsibility for gathering and retaining the decedent's key documents, including:

- The original will and any subsequent, revised wills or codicils
- Trust agreements
- Power of Attorney (POA) Note: In some states, certain instructions in a health care power of attorney may need to be carried out after the decedent's death. While other powers of attorney cease to be valid after an individual's death, you may still want to gather those documents and make sure that all institutions know that the agent named in the power of attorney, if it is someone

other than the executor, no longer has any legal authority to transact business on behalf of the decedent.

- The decedent's birth certificate and Social Security card
- Check register
- Savings and certificate of deposit account passbooks
- Stock and bond certificates
- Insurance policies
- Real property deeds and titles
- Personal property titles
- Marriage and divorce certificates
- Military papers
- Certified death certificates to file claims for life insurance, survivor benefits and to change the title of property and financial accounts

If you're unable to locate originals or certified copies of marriage or birth certificates, divorce agreements, military service papers or Social Security cards, check with your local Department of Vital Records.

■ Establish Critical Records

Keep an organized list of all property, income, debts and expenses of the estate. This documentation will prove useful when closing the estate.

■ Submitting the Will to Probate

Probate is the legal process used to prove the validity of a written will. To begin, contact the clerk of the probate court (sometimes also referred to as the Surrogate's Court or Register or Registry of wills) in your county for the necessary procedures. (In some cases, the deceased may have lived in one county and the executor in another.) It is important to authorize distribution of property according to the will's specific provisions. If you need to probate the will, you may need to hire an attorney to assist you. It is not necessary to use the same attorney who drafted the will.

Once the will is filed with the probate court, the court will formally appoint the executor named in the will and issue Letters of Testamentary, which authorize the executor to begin settlement procedures. The executor is also responsible for collecting monies owed to the decedent, paying the decedent's debts, managing and distributing their property and submitting a final accounting to the court.

When an individual dies without a will, the process of distributing a decedent's estate is known as estate administration. Each state has laws of descent that dictate the distribution of an estate, if there is no valid will. These laws usually provide for the surviving spouse and children to receive shares of the estate. The first step is to have the court issue Letters of Administration authorizing the appointed administrator to settle the estate.

Certain assets are not subject to probate because they are held in ways that result in the passing of ownership directly to an intended beneficiary upon the death of the owner without going through any probate process.

One of the most common non-probate assets is a home held by spouses jointly with a right of survivorship. The property automatically becomes the sole property of the surviving owner upon the death of decedent.

Individuals may also own bank or brokerage accounts with a "right of survivorship" or another form of ownership known as "payable on death" or "transfer on death" registration. In states which recognize POD and TOD arrangements, such bank or brokerage accounts will transfer as quickly and easily as if they had been owned in a right of survivorship.

The other widely-owned class of assets that can be transferred at death without probate court involvement are assets such as life insurance and retirement accounts. These assets may pass under the terms of an individual's will, but usually only if the individual names their estate as the beneficiary. Otherwise, life insurance proceeds and monies from retirement accounts will be paid directly to the named beneficiary.

Until the probate process is completed, bank accounts and other assets may be frozen, safe deposit boxes sealed and other steps taken to protect the interests of heirs and to conserve assets subject to estate taxes. Sometimes, exceptions are made. For example, banks will often allow a surviving spouse to withdraw funds to meet daily living expenses until the estate is settled. Should the bank refuse to allow any assets to be withdrawn, the court can order the release of assets from the estate.

■ Contacting Heirs and Beneficiaries

Follow through to make sure the attorney and/or the court notifies all persons who are named in the will and likely to receive assets from the estate. Retain a list of their names, addresses, birth dates, Social Security numbers and telephone numbers for paperwork and such.

Some state laws require your personal representative to publish a death notice in your local paper. The death notice serves as a public notice of your estate's probate and enables people who think they have an interest in the estate (such as creditors) to file a claim against your estate within a specified time period.

■ Establishing an Estate Account

When necessary (either required by the court procedural rules or your bank or due to the sheer volume of assets and/or beneficiaries), the executor will open an estate checking account. The estate checking account is used to combine all liquid assets of the decedent and pay the expenses of the estate. Please note that in order to open an estate checking account, you (or your attorney) will need to obtain a Taxpayer Identification number (TIN), similar to an individual Social Security number. A TIN can only be obtained through the I.R.S. There is no fee for the TIN, and if you call the I.R.S. with a completed Form SS-4 on hand (rather than mail the document), the TIN will be given to you during the call. Before obtaining the TIN, you should consult your attorney.

■ Inventorying the Assets

Make a list of the assets of the estate. This would include all real and personal property as well as the titles and/or deeds for each asset.

■ Ensuring that Property is Properly Insured

Insurance policies that protect the real and personal property held by the estate, including fire, theft, casualty and collision insurance, should be maintained and even improved if necessary. Be sure to notify the various insurance carriers of any changes in coverage. Furthermore, depending on state probate procedures, the executor or administrator may be required to obtain a bond before Letters of Testamentary/Administration are issued.

If it is appropriate to change the names on bank accounts, mutual funds, stock and other financial accounts, bring a copy of the death certificate to each financial institution. Stocks or bonds bequeathed to particular people or entities by the decedent's will must be re-registered in the beneficiaries' names.

The title to real estate may also need to be updated to reflect the change in ownership.

■ Take Caution When Changing Names on Accounts

Before making any name changes on accounts, be sure to check with legal counsel, as your own estate plan may be adversely affected. A simple name change or even the innocent act of cashing a check payable in joint name or solely to the decedent can abolish the opportunity for certain post-mortem plans such as the process of disclaiming assets.

■ Collect Outstanding Receivables

All debts owed to decedent or the estate may be collected now or may need to have payments redirected to the estate. Either way, these are among the assets that comprise the estate.

Collect unpaid receivables such as salary, insurance and employee benefits. Review the deceased's personal records to ensure that the estate receives all benefits due from his or her employer and various insurance companies. Contact the benefits office of both current and past employers for more information.

■ Valuing the Assets

Arrange for these assets to be appraised at the date of decedent's death. If there is any one item valued at over $3,000 or a collection of items with a combined value of $10,000, an appraisal is required and must be attached to the estate tax return.

You might also try to project the value of such assets in the future; say six to 12 months from that date. Highly collectible items such as sports memorabilia, artwork and other possessions may naturally increase in value over time or may have their value tied to a key event such as a sports record or the death of the artist. Anticipating any change to the value of each item—either higher or lower—will help you make better, more informed decisions.

For the more valuable or unique possessions, you may consider hiring an appraiser to valuate the item for public sale. If there are a tremendous number of items in the collection, you may consider donating the entire collection to a museum or not-for-profit organization. You could also consider holding an auction or estate sale or trying your hand at an online auction. eBay and other online auction sites often require a photo, brief description and a minimum price you'd be willing to accept. Once the sale has been made, you will be responsible for packing and shipping the item to the buyer.

If you are reluctant to handle the online auction yourself, you might consider hiring a third-party asset liquidator. Be prepared to pay 30 to 50 percent of the final purchase price as a commission.

■ Notifying Creditors and Paying Appropriate Bills

Notify all creditors in writing of the decedent's passing. Prior to paying outstanding debts, consult an attorney since only those debts incurred by the decedent alone are considered debts of the estate.

In those cases where there are no probate assets, the estate is said to be bankrupt; therefore any outstanding unsecured or non-medical debts may not be able to be satisfied. Keep in mind that paying debts, such as funeral expenses, attorney's fees, estate administration expenses and various taxes, are given priority by the state.

Also note that for those decedents living in a community property state, a spouse is considered liable for any marital debt, even if the debt were solely incurred by the decedent. Consult an attorney for clarification on these issues and <u>before</u> paying <u>any</u> debts.

■ Determining Federal and State ESTATE TAX Liability

Calculate the total value of the gross estate and compare it to the current I.R.S. exemption. Note that the gross estate is different than the probate estate. Often times the gross estate will include life insurance proceeds (even though they are payable directly to beneficiaries), other assets with designated beneficiaries and jointly-owned property with a right of survivorship.

If the gross estate is larger than the current exemption, the I.R.S. requires the executor or administrator of the estate to file Federal Estate Tax Form 706 <u>within nine months of the decedent's death.</u> If additional time is needed to complete the estate tax return, a Form 4768 can be filed on or before the due date requesting a six-month extension of time to file the return. NOTE: The extension only extends the time to file the return, not the time to pay any estate tax if there is tax due. Also ask your attorney or tax preparer if there is a state filing requirement that must be fulfilled.

■ Determining Federal and State Estate INCOME TAX Liability

Gross income includes dividends, interest, rents, royalties, capital gains and income from businesses, partnerships, trusts and other sources. If the estate has a gross income of $600 or more during a taxable year, the I.R.S. requires the executor or administrator to file Federal Trust and Estate Income Tax Form 1041. An estate income tax return (Form 1041) may also be necessary. This return would segregate income earned before date of death, and income earned after date of death. Again, ask your attorney or tax preparer if there is a state requirement.

■ Filing a Federal Estate Tax Return

A federal estate tax return must be filed <u>within nine months after decedent's death</u>—if the estate exceeds the "applicable credit" amount that otherwise excludes the estate from federal taxes. Consult an attorney for the most current guidelines.

■ Distributing Assets

Consult with appropriate heirs and beneficiaries about the orderly distribution of estate assets. Generally, executors may not distribute the estate assets until after the period for creditors to make claims expires, which can be <u>as long as one year after the death.</u>

■ Be Aware of Disclaimers

Consider possible disclaimers of beneficial or joint interests by the surviving spouse or other beneficiaries. Some beneficiaries may disclaim amounts that they may be due to receive from the estate. This option should be considered early in the process to preserve the beneficiary's ability to disclaim.

■ Prepare and Distribute a Final Report to the Beneficiaries

The executor needs to create an account of his actions and then needs to ask the beneficiaries to release him from any liability to the beneficiary. As executor or executrix, it helps to know about this up-front because you may want to be better organized in your recordkeeping from the start of the process.

■ Processing a Living Trust

If the deceased had a Living Trust, the estate settlement will be different from that of someone who had a traditional will. A Living Trust, properly called a revocable inter vivos trust, is often used in conjunction with a will to avoid either probate in the event of death, or to establish guardianship in the event of incapacitation.

At the death of the grantor—the person who funded the trust—the Living Trust becomes irrevocable and the named assets are distributed according to the terms of the trust. Title transfers upon death generally are easier with trust assets than assets titled in the decedent's name alone, since typically the survivor simply needs to produce a copy of the death certificate and trust document to transfer property. Thus, in many cases, distribution of assets from a trust do not require court supervision (i.e. no probate). An exception would be if the decedent had a "pour-over" provision in the will directing any assets that are not titled to the trust be put into the trust at his or her death. These assets will still be subject to probate and directed to the trust by a decedent's will.

Whether probated or not, assets of the Living Trust are still included in the value of the estate for purposes of estate income and inheritance tax.

Nonetheless, trusts are an excellent tool for proper management and distribution of assets. Furthermore, trusts usually do not become a "public document," thus providing privacy to your family.

The checklist found in this chapter may not cover every responsibility. To properly complete the entire estate process, the executor and survivor should always work closely with an attorney.

To-Do List

____ Gather all significant documents of the decedent.

____ Keep an organized list of all property, income, debts and expenses of the estate.

____ Contact the clerk of the probate court to process estate.

____ Ensure that an executor or administrator is formally named by the court.

____ If required, obtain a bond before Letters of Testamentary or Administration are issued.

____ Contact all heirs and beneficiaries.

____ Obtain a Taxpayer Identification Number (TIN) and establish a bank account for the estate.

____ Ensure that all real and personal property owned by the estate is fully insured.

____ Collect all debts owed to the estate or have payments redirected to the estate.

____ Inventory and value the high-ticket items and make a decision whether to liquidate and when.

____ Notify all known creditors in writing and place a death notice of the decedent's death to see if there are any additional creditors that may come forward.

____ File state and federal tax returns with nine months.

____ Distribute assets but ensure that there are adequate monies retained to cover taxes or closing costs.

____ Process the Living Trust, if applicable.

Notes

Chapter 8

Attending to
Personal Affairs

Tending to the personal affairs of the decedent can be quite emotional. There is something about the finality of these simple tasks that make them a bit daunting. With that in mind, in addition to having someone you trust with you when you're dealing with all of those personal affairs, you may also want to delegate some of the following tasks to trusted friends or family.

■ Deciding What to Do with Clothing

Start by sorting items into three piles. Items you know you want to keep, items you can let go and those of which you are not sure. Then, put away the items you wish to keep, let go of the second pile and set aside the remaining pile for later. Repeat this process if necessary.

After sorting through their personal possessions and distributing meaningful items to family and friends, it's time to look at other avenues for putting their remaining possessions to good use. One of the nicest ways to honor your loved one's life is to donate the belongings so that they might make a difference for others. Coats, clothes, eyeglasses, shoes and boots, games, vehicles, etc. can all be donated to worthy causes in your community.

Start by choosing charities that your loved one might have had some affinity with and then add others that would have also appealed to them. There are also charities with specific programs that may appeal to you. For example, the Lion's Club is always looking for used eyeglasses to repair and distribute to needy individuals.

Dress for Success (www.DressforSuccess.org) and Career Gear (www.CareerGear.org) are not-for-profits that operate an impressive clothing exchange to help low-income women and men, respectively, suit up for job interviews and be positioned for success.

If you are affiliated with a church or temple that has a second-hand store, donation is a wonderful way to support their ongoing community outreach programs. Your local United Way can give you a comprehensive list of charities in your area.

In order for the beneficiary to receive a tax deduction for the contribution of the deceased's clothing, they must estimate the value of each item. Check for the original sales receipts or credit card receipts, if available, to gauge the value. This is especially important for the more expensive items.

■ Decide What to Do with Excess Medical Equipment and Supplies

If this death occurred after a long illness, chances are that your house is filled with a wide variety of half-empty prescription bottles, unused medical supplies and medical equipment. The longer these items remain in your home, the longer you may be reminded of your loved one's struggle to survive. Consider putting these items to good use by donating them.

Medical equipment can often be donated to the local volunteer ambulance corps or town hall who will provide it to citizens of your town free-of-charge.

You can also consider donating such items to a local clinic. Doctors Without Borders is an international organization that provides medical care to some of the poorest villages and towns around the globe. Unlike U.S. medical facilities that are mandated by Food & Drug Administration guidelines, this organization will gladly take that half-used box of latex gloves, gauze bandages and whatever else you have. For more information about how you can participate, visit their website at www.DoctorsWithoutBorders.org.

If money is tight, you may also consider selling the equipment you have on eBay or other online auction sites. You will still be making it possible for someone to purchase the equipment at a very attractive price.

■ Eliminating Solicitors

Founded in 1917, the Direct Marketing Association is the oldest and largest national trade organization serving the direct marketing industry. To remove the decedent's name from mailing lists, magazines, catalogs, newsletters, book/music clubs, etc. go to its website at www.dmaconsumers.org or send a letter to:

> DMA Mail Preference Service
> P.O. Box 9008
> Farmingdale, NY 11735-9008
>
> AND
>
> DMA Mail Preference Service
> P.O. Box 643
> Carmel, NY 10512

■ Eliminating Unsolicited Credit Card Applications

Everyone is used to getting regular solicitations from credit card companies and even pre-approved credit cards from banks and finance companies. There is a very easy way to reduce both and even save some trees in the process. Now you can make a single phone call to (888) 5-OPT-OUT or (888) 567-8688, a toll-free number established by the credit reporting industry.

When you call this number, you may request to have your name and address removed from national credit bureau lists that are sold to the credit industry. The three national credit reporting agencies—Experian (formerly TRW), Trans Union, and Equifax—will remove your name for a two-year period from any list provided to others relating to any potential consumer credit transaction that you do not initiate. You will have to provide some personal information and follow the directions you receive from a pre-recorded message. If you follow these directions, your name should be removed within five business days.

You may even ask to have your name permanently removed by requesting that the credit bureau send to you an "election form." This form, when filled out and returned by you, will remove your name and address from credit bureau mailing lists until you notify them that you want to be placed on these lists again.

Federal and state laws include many other provisions to protect consumers. Watch for future Consumer Alerts for more information concerning your rights as a consumer when seeking or being offered credit services.

■ Reducing Phone Solicitations

Everyone hates getting those annoying phone calls, especially at dinnertime. Now there is a simple way to have the deceased's name removed from telemarketing lists—for just $1.00. The Direct Marketing Association (DMA) has also created a "Deceased Do Not Contact List" (DDNC) for the sole purpose of removing names and addresses of deceased individuals from any marketing lists.

When you register a name on the DDNC, the person's name, address, phone number and e-mail address is placed in a special do not contact file. All DMA members are required to eliminate these individuals from their prospecting campaigns. The service is also available to non-members of the DMA so that all marketers may take advantage of this service to eliminate names. You may register online by going to www.dmaconsumers.org.

If you do not have Internet access, send a letter to the Telephone Preference Service (TPS), a service sponsored by the Direct Marketing Association (DMA).

DMA Telephone Preference Service (TPS)
PO Box 9014
Farmingdale, NY 11735
www.dmaconsumers.org

PLUS

DMA Telephone Preference Service
P.O. Box 1559
Carmel, NY 10512
www.dmaconsumers.org

There is also a very straightforward way to have both your own name and the name of deceased removed from these phone lists. Simply call toll-free (888) 382-1222 and follow the prompts to register your phone numbers on the National Do Not Call Registry. Or go to www.donotcall.gov. Your registration will be effective for a minimum of five years.

■ Reducing e-mail Solicitations and SPAM

Whether or not we like it, SPAM or unwanted e-mail solicitations are something we all have had to learn to deal with. But, it is important to have the decedent's name removed from such lists used by vendors. Contact the Direct Marketing Association online at www.thedma.org and www.e-mps.org.

■ Handling e-mail Accounts

Today, so much communication takes place over the Internet that e-mail addresses have become as significant as U.S. mailing addresses. You may selectively use the e-mail address book to determine names of people who should be notified of the decedent's death. Consider keeping that e-mail account open for several months following the death. At this time, you may also consider obtaining a second e-mail account to gradually redirect important correspondence as well as further weed out junk e-mail and undesired web-based solicitations.

■ Transferring Vehicle Ownership

If you are going to transfer the ownership of any vehicles owned by the decedent, you must first locate the title for each. If the title is lost, apply for a duplicate title in the name of the deceased. The duplicate title may then be used to transfer vehicle ownership.

In many states, ownership of registered vehicles may automatically be transferred to the surviving spouse or children under age 21. A surviving spouse or child transferring a registration to their own name may receive credit for the unexpired portion of the deceased's registration. The survivors may also keep the same license plates, however, title and transaction fees still apply.

When there is no will, estate, surviving spouse or surviving minor child, the next of kin may complete the transfer. A copy of the death certificate is required.

For more information about the specific process for transferring ownership, contact your local Department of Motor Vehicles.

■ Change or Cancel Utility Accounts

Utilities include gas, electricity, water/sewer, garbage collection, cable, Internet access, etc. If the decedent's name is on the utility account, contact the company to change or cancel the account. They often don't need proof of death to make this change.

■ Redirecting Property Taxes

If the decedent and the survivor jointly owned property, the estate will likely transfer the property tax to the survivor.

■ Modifying Home and Auto Insurance

If necessary, contact the appropriate insurers to modify accounts with proper names. Check the mortgage or car title for the name of the insurance company. You will not need proof of death to modify the name of the insured.

■ Change or Cancel Other Accounts

Where there are existing accounts with a grocery store, electronic toll collection services such as EZ Pass and Fast Lane, pharmacies, libraries or video stores, contact the appropriate company to cancel any accounts no longer used or update accounts with name of the surviving spouse or child. You don't need proof of death to do this.

■ Complete Decedent's Unfinished Business

If the unfortunate death was quick or unexpected, it is very likely that he or she left a bit of unfinished business. As the executor, it is important for you complete, return, cancel or pick-up any of the various plans or activities in process. On the next page, we've started a list and given you space to add other items.

To-Do List

_____ Consider donating clothes, eyeglasses and medical equipment and supplies or selling items.

_____ Contact the DMA to stop unwanted phone, mail, e-mail and credit card solicitations.

_____ Transfer vehicle ownership.

_____ Change or cancel utility accounts.

_____ Modify home and auto insurance policies.

_____ Pick up dry cleaning or tailoring, shoes, skis, etc.

_____ Return library books, videos, DVDs. (Note: Any fines are a debt of the estate.)

_____ Return any recent purchases that are unused or no longer needed. Cancel purchases on layaway.

_____ Cancel any future appointments with doctors, dentists, or other services.

_____ Cancel vacations or any other pre-planned events.

_____ Cancel open prescription and retail credit card accounts.

_____ _____

_____ _____

_____ _____

_____ _____

_____ _____

Notes

Chapter 9

Avoiding Identity Theft

Identity theft is the fastest-growing crime in the world. It occurs when someone obtains and uses your personal information without your knowledge to commit fraud or theft. While a number of companies put security standards and procedures in place to prevent unauthorized access to customer information, you should still take your own precautions. Here are some steps you can take to avoid becoming a victim of identity theft:

■ Protect Your Personal Information

- Avoid carrying your Social Security number and driver's license together in your wallet.
- Shred papers using cross-cut shredders— especially pre-approved credit card offers.
- Drop paid bills directly into U.S. Postal mailboxes —not in your home mailbox.
- Collect mail within two hours of delivery.
- Don't ever sign blank forms.
- Verify beneficiary information on life insurance and retirement accounts on a regular basis.

■ Protect Your Electronic Information

- Protect any web page User ID and passwords by using a combination of letters and numbers. Store your codes in a locked drawer and change them often. Don't use your Social Security number, date of birth, or mother's maiden name as a PIN or password. Should anyone obtain your PINs or passwords, they can obtain the kind of personal information that leads to identity theft. Never carry this information with you.

- Control access to your computer by setting up a user password. Remember that your browser history files will automatically record recent web pages visited as well as specific access information. If someone were to have access to your personal computer, they may also have the same access to web accounts previously established by you or the decedent.

■ Establish More than One e-mail

Use one for personal correspondence with friends and family and another for online transactions. This way you can delete the latter in case you become suspicious or simply get bombarded with unsolicited e-mail or SPAM.

■ Don't Go "Phishing"

Never respond to unsolicited e-mail from banks, credit card companies, online auction or PayPal sites asking you to verify or update personal and account information. Scammers are constantly casting about for people's financial information by luring unsuspecting victims through a technique called "phishing."

Phishing is a high-tech scam that uses SPAM to trick consumers into disclosing their credit card numbers, bank account information, Social Security numbers, passwords and other sensitive personal information. Consumers who provide their financial information in response to an unsolicited e-mail could be at risk of identity theft.

■ Protect Against Hackers

Get a computer firewall and keep your virus and spyware software up-to-date to guard against outsiders getting into your computer system remotely.

■ Monitor Activity on Credit Cards and Bank Accounts

Monitor credit card bills and credit reports for unauthorized transactions. If you are a victim of identify fraud, you will quickly find purchases or withdrawals you never made on your credit card or debit account. Review your bank and credit card

■ Keep on Eye on Automated Double Billings

Many people now use their credit cards to pay for their satellite TV or cable, EZ Pass, Netflix and other services that have a monthly service charge. As you check your credit card bills, be on the lookout for double billings or the same debit amount to the same service provider appearing twice in one month or one quarter.

■ Report Fraud Immediately

The first line of defense is to simply become more aware of identity theft and more aggressive in personally protecting yourself. A 2003 Federal Trade Commission report said 26 percent of all identity theft victims discover the misuse within one week to one month after it begins, but 12 percent take over six months to discover the problem.

The faster you report any incidence of fraud, the faster the bank or credit card company can start to close accounts and clear your name right away. Furthermore, you should request that a fraud alert be placed on your credit report file so the credit bureau must contact you before any new credit can be approved.

Contact each of the credit reporting agencies listed below:

Equifax	(800) 525-6285
Experian	(888) 397-3742
Trans Union	(800) 680-7289

■ Considering Purchasing Fraud Protection

In addition to the precautions mentioned above, you may wish to consider identity fraud protection via property and casualty insurance carrier or implementing services such as those available through www.identityfraud.com , www.trustedid.com, www.lifelock.com and many others.

■ Stay Informed

For more information, you may also contact the Federal Trade Commission's ID Theft Hotline at 1-877-IDTHEFT or 1-877-438-4338 toll-free or visit www.consumer.gov/idtheft. The site contains helpful information for consumers and businesses on a variety of topics, including "phishing" scams, telecommunications fraud, Internet fraud, and the theft of printed documents with personal information, as well as protecting employees from identity theft in the workplace.

The site also contains valuable consumer information on the steps to take if and when you find yourself a victim of identity theft.

statements carefully as soon as you receive them. Report any unauthorized purchases to the credit card company immediately. Chances are you will not be required to pay for them.

■ Order Copies of Your Credit Report Every Year

Because identity theft has become so rampant, federal law now allows you to obtain a FREE credit report online, by phone or through the mail every year.

- Request your credit report online at: www.annualcreditreport.com
- Request your credit report by phone. Call 1-877-322-8228 (toll-free) to request your credit reports by phone. You will go through a simple verification process and then your reports will be mailed to you.
- Request your credit report by mail. You can request your credit report by mail by filling out the request form at the end of this chapter and mailing it to:

> Annual Credit Report Request Service
> P.O. Box 105281
> Atlanta, GA 30348-5281

■ Cancel Any Credit Cards You Don't Use

To-Do List

_____ Avoid carrying your Social Security card and driver's license together.

_____ Use a cross-cut shredder to dispose of credit card offers, credit card checks and personal information.

_____ Change user IDs and passwords regularly. Use a combination of letters and numbers, but never use your Social Security number, mother's maiden name or date of birth.

_____ Establish more than one e-mail account—one for online transactions, one for personal communications.

_____ Never respond to unsolicited e-mails from banks, credit card companies, online auction sites, PayPal asking you to verify personal information.

_____ Install a computer firewall. Keep your virus and spyware software up-to-date.

_____ Monitor activity on banks and credit cards. Report fraud or identity theft immediately.

_____ Order copies of your credit reports at least once a year.

_____ Cancel any credit cards you don't use.

_____ Keep an eye out for double, automated billings on utilities, mortgage and car loans.

_____ Consider purchasing fraud insurance.

Notes

Chapter 10

Proactive Planning: Ensure You Leave Behind a Meaningful Legacy

Whether your experiences have been positive, negative or both, you have certainly come to appreciate the abundance of complexities that arise in the aftermath of death. When the time is right, I suggest you reflect on your experiences and think about how your loved ones will cope when you die. Thinking about your own mortality is not easy, especially in light of the fact that you just lost someone dear to you. And, if you are like most people, you also might be thinking "I am still young and healthy" or "I'm too busy." Well, there may be truth to some or all of these objections, but they are not good enough reasons to leave your survivors with more questions than answers.

In these final chapters, you will learn about personal legacy planning and traditional estate planning. It is my belief that both of them are necessary to ensure that you leave behind a meaningful legacy.

Before we get started, let's talk about the difference between the two. As you may know, estate planning addresses your material assets and possessions of financial value, and your wishes for how they will be disbursed in the event you should pass away or cannot communicate for yourself. Estate planning is accomplished with tools such as a legal will, trusts, powers of attorney, health care proxies, etc.

Your true wealth, however, is not measured in just dollars and material assets—and that is where personal legacy planning comes in. Personal legacy planning addresses your non-material assets, possessions of emotional value. This includes your values, life lessons, memories, and final wishes—information that is too valuable to risk being lost. It is a perfect complement to your estate plan.

Let's get more specific. A couple of years ago, Bob called and told me that he had terminal cancer. He wanted to proactively document everything he could think of (both personal and practical) that would be beneficial to his wife. He had already taken care of his estate plan and made sure she was okay financially—but he was more concerned about her emotional well-being and her ability to move forward after he died.

When I told him about the concept of personal legacy planning, he was relieved. He was able to document practical information about things such as his funeral arrangements, maintaining the household, his plans for the kids, and the location of important documents. He was also delighted to share important personal messages such as thoughts about how and why he loved his wife, favorite memories about their family vacations to Florida, his views on religion, and other philosophical thoughts that he felt could positively impact future generations. The legacy planning process helped Bob gain clarity and confidence that everything that mattered to him would be passed on to those he loved.

Imagine the peace of mind Bob had, knowing that instead of a tangled web of unanswered questions, his loved ones would have all the information they would need and long for.

Although personal legacy planning is not a prerequisite for establishing an estate plan, it is most beneficial when done first. By creating a legacy plan, you become much more in tune with what matters most to you. Obviously, this can have a significant influence on how you put together your estate plan. So, with that in mind, let's start by exploring the four steps to creating a meaningful legacy plan.

■ Get Your House in Order

In the hours and days after death, your survivors will be asked to produce the kind of documentation listed below. Take a few hours, now, to start getting organized so the burden on your survivors will be eased at a very difficult time. This will also give you an opportunity to ensure that important documents like your will, health care proxy and durable power of attorney are accurate and up-to-date. This is also the time to confirm beneficiary information on retirement accounts. And it is also appropriate for you to sit down with your trusted financial advisor and/or attorney to make sure everything is exactly as you want it to be. There is clearly a danger of waiting too long, of waiting until an illness has impaired your judgment, and placing all of your plans at risk.

Here is a list of 38 vital documents you should update and organize:

Personal Documents
- List of prescription drugs and vaccinations
- Organ donor card
- Living will/health care proxy
- Durable power of attorney
- Will
- Prenuptial/postnuptial agreements
- Legacy plan
- Birth certificates/adoption papers
- Death certificates
- Social Security card
- Copy of driver's license
- Passports
- Marriage license
- Divorce decrees

- Military papers/discharge papers
- Pet records

Property Documents
- Deeds, titles and title insurance for home
- Title and insurance for auto(s)
- Deeds, titles and title insurance for other property
- Videotape/DVD inventory of house
- Backup DVD or tape of computer hard drive
- Copy of homeowner's insurance
- Coins, jewelry, etc.
- Service contracts

Financial Documents
- Life insurance policies
- Disability insurance policies
- Long-term care policies
- Stock/Bond certificates
- Private loan papers
- Business and buy-sell agreements
- School tax records
- Cost basis data
- Income and gift tax returns
- Copy of employment contract
- Pension plan records
- Copies of credit cards and toll-free numbers
- List of website user IDs and passwords
- Copy of receipts for home improvements

■ Share Your Values

A true legacy is about much more than just being organized and leaving money. It should cover all facets of your life: your values, traditions, life lessons, history, and final wishes. By documenting these things, you to share the softer, more personal matters with generations to come.

Here are some sample questions you might want to consider documenting answers to:

- Describe your background, life history and favorite family memories.
- What are your most important principles and values?
- What are your religious/spiritual beliefs and what do they mean to you?
- What are your hopes for the future for your family?
- How did you meet your spouse/partner and what was the first date like?
- What is your favorite childhood memory?
- How do you define true success?

Sharing answers to these types of questions provides your loved ones and future generations a window to your soul and a better understanding of who you are.

■ Document the Details

Documenting the details is about recording important practical information about your life. Practical information about things such as instructions on how to raise the children, funeral and burial arrangements, organ donation, pet and home care, locations of key documents, and more. This information complements many of the fine points not included in other end-of-life documents (e.g., a will or health care proxy).

Here are some things you might want to consider documenting details about:

People to be Notified—For each, list name, address, phone numbers and relationship. Add a brief description of how you met each person to pave the way for communication, cooperation and meaningful participation in a celebration of your life.

Important Business/Personal Contacts—Include the names of your physician, clergy, attorney, accountant, insurance agent, financial advisor, banker, supervisor at work, etc.

Personal Documents/Information—Include date of birth, location of birth certificate, Social Security number, data on any previous marriages, armed forces service and discharge information, names and contact information for relatives, etc.

Benefits from Employment—Names of previous employers, dates of hire and termination, health insurance providers, flex account contributions, elected benefits, etc.

Bank and Investment Accounts—List account numbers paired with financial institutions, location of regularly visited branches, branch manager's name and phone number, number and location of safe deposit box and keys, etc.

Medical and Disability Insurance—This information will be critical for your executor as well as the person named as your health care proxy. List insurance providers and account numbers along with coverage information and the location of the policies.

Credit, Debit and ATM Cards—This is an enlightening exercise for everyone to do. List all credit cards by type, account number, financial institution and credit limit. If you have established passwords or Personal Identification Numbers (PIN) for any of your accounts, including ATM cards, leave instructions as to the secure location where those can be found.

Tax-Related Information—Provide instructions as to where copies of past tax returns are located and the name and phone number of your tax preparer.

Your Living will or Health Care Proxy—Provide instructions as to where copies are located and make certain that copies are easily accessible by your doctors or any other caretakers.

Special Final Requests—Admittedly, this is a catch-all, but you'd be surprised at the number of things that could potentially fit in this category, including all those things that you may have deemed too insignificant or too private to include in your will.

Here are a few more things you might also consider providing details about:

- Final wishes about funeral arrangements, organ donation, autopsy, etc.
- Family history
- Household maintenance
- Care instructions for children and pets
- Computer passwords
- Catalog of collectibles and their current value
- Personal business ventures
- Commercial and residential real estate
- Trust funds
- Personal debtors and creditors
- Homeowners and mortgage insurance
- Vehicle/Boat insurance
- Life insurance policies

By filling out this information, you will remove much of the burden that would otherwise fall upon your survivors and save them hours of tedious work.

■ Live with Purpose

Create a "bucket list" of goals you would like to accomplish before you "kick the bucket." It will inspire you as you move forward with your life. Include things you've always dreamt of doing, as well as short-term goals like becoming more organized. Always keep your list current by adding, editing or marking complete any item on your list.

Imagine the impact you could have on future generations. You could inspire your great-grandchild to accomplish the same things that you did. Who knows, you might start a family tradition of climbing the high peaks in the Adirondack Mountains or visiting underdeveloped countries to help mankind!

By completing these four items, you can rest assured knowing that you will leave behind a meaningful legacy rather than a tangled web of unanswered questions.

If you would prefer some guidance with planning your legacy, so that you are confident that it is done properly, consider seeking the assistance of a legacy advisor trained by Plan Your Legacy. Legacy advisors who are members of Plan Your Legacy have access to

Breadcrumbs™, an online software program designed specifically for creating meaningful legacy plans. It covers all of the information mentioned here and many other important details. The software also has a unique delivery method that ensures your legacy plan is delivered to the right people at the right time. For more information, go to www.planyourlegacy.com.

Notes

Chapter 11

Proactive Planning: Formalizing Your Estate Plan and Final Wishes

Now, let's talk about how you shall address your material assets, possessions of financial value and your final wishes. My intent here is to explain the basics of estate planning and share some practical tips. However, as you might suspect, estate planning can be complicated. So, in addition to empowering yourself with the following information, be sure to seek the professional counsel of a well-respected estate planning attorney. For suggestions on how to choose a good attorney, please refer back to Chapter 1.

■ Draft or Modify Your Will

If the decedent was the first beneficiary to inherit under your will, you must designate a new one. If one dies without a properly executed will, that is they die intestate, the courts will determine to whom the assets will be distributed to.

If most or all of the property passed to you as a result of rights of survivorship, beneficiary designations, etc., you may want to consult with an estate planning attorney to determine if your estate is sufficiently large that it would be advantageous to replace your will with a Living Trust.

■ Draft a Living Will or a Health Care Proxy

A living will is an advance directive which presents your wishes for treatment and care when you are not able to make your own decisions. This document is only followed when you have a terminal condition and only deals with life-prolonging procedures.

The second type of advance directive—often called a Durable Power of Attorney for health care or health care proxy—covers those situations when you can't make treatment decisions for yourself. If you wish, the person to whom you give a durable power of attorney for health care can make any decisions about your health care that you could have made yourself, including life-prolonging measures. Contact your attorney for more information.

■ Adopt a Durable Power of Attorney

A Power of Attorney will authorize someone else to handle your financial affairs if you are unable to do so. Contact your attorney for more information.

■ Identify Beneficiaries/Owners When Possible

Where you have the opportunity, I suggest you assign your assets to individuals by naming them as beneficiaries. You can name beneficiaries to life insurance policies and retirement accounts—both individual retirement accounts (IRAs) and employer-sponsored plans. For non-retirement accounts, check to see if a transfer on death (TOD) or payable on death (POD) contract is available. This will allow you to name a beneficiary just like you would on an IRA or other type of retirement account. At death, assets with designated beneficiaries will transfer directly to your beneficiaries without going through probate, saving time and attorney's fees.

■ Consider Changing Individual into Jointly-Held Accounts

As you saw, whenever there are accounts that are jointly held by one or more persons, those assets transfer quickly and easily to the other person named on the account. If you are planning on transferring your cash assets to a known individual, consider simply adding that person's name to the account at the appropriate time. Once again, you should check with your attorney, as this action may constitute a gift and contradict with your existing post-mortem planning.

■ Consider Crafting a New Estate Plan

Many individuals don't know how much property they own or whether it is potentially subject to federal estate tax or state inheritance tax. It pays to consult a accountant, attorney or other tax professional who can help you sort out these difficult and complex estate issues.

■ Consider a Purposeful Trust™

Most documents do very little to convey the real human caring and concerns of the clients for whom they are prepared. Lost in all the legalese is the love parents and grandparents feel for their children and grandchildren, the faith they have in their descendants' potential to grow and develop, and the hope they hold for the future.

If you want to be sure that you are leaving your heirs more than money, and that the assets you leave them will have a positive impact rather than a corrosive influence in their lives, you may want to consider a revolutionary new planning technique called the Purposeful Trust™. Children, grandchildren and other beneficiaries, upon reading a Purposeful Trust™ will know it really is your document because they will hear your voice and appreciate more deeply the financial bequests, priceless heirlooms and lasting legacies, life lessons and wisdom you have left them.

A financial planner or attorney who has been trained to capture your voice through a technique called Purposeful Conversations can assist you with the process to help you think clearly about which of the Seven Secrets of the Purposeful Trust™ you might want to incorporate in your planning. The experience is simple, enjoyable and very gratifying.

■ Pre-Arrange Your Funeral

Recently, I attended a pre-planned funeral. Not only had this dear friend purchased his casket and burial plot, he also planned every detail of his funeral. He picked the person to deliver the eulogy and identified the songs, poems and readings for the service. It was immediately gratifying to know that he was remembered in a way that truly reflected his beliefs, his tastes and his life.

It is important, however, to include your family in this process. After all, they will be the ones directly affected and emotionally touched by the service. You should also let them know that they are welcome to change the plans if it means that they will better represent everybody's wishes at the time of your death. Also keep in mind that it is prudent to review these plans every two to four years so they reflect your current desires.

Another reason to take control of your funeral arrangements is to ease the burden carried by your survivors and close friends. A typical funeral can cost between $6,000 and $10,000. If you don't make these major purchasing decisions in advance, your family will be asked to make them for you at a time of acute grief. You may be experiencing that in your situation right now. Survivors may feel guilty about cutting costs. And they may be overwhelmed by the number of decisions they will need to make. Pre-planning your funeral is one of the best ways to avoid possible confusion over the type of arrangements you'd want and you may also save money.

The best way to pre-arrange a funeral is to sit down and talk with a trusted funeral director in your community. The Funeral Rule, enforced by the Federal Trade Commission, requires funeral directors to offer free consultations to give you advice, itemized prices and other information about their goods and services.

Once you've made your pre-arrangements, keep a copy of your plan and any pertinent paperwork in a safe place. Also, inform a close friend or relative about the arrangements you have made and where the information may be found.

Pre-arranging your funeral does not require you to prepay for it. While I am a huge proponent of pre-arranging your funeral, I often tell people that before prepaying for a funeral, carefully evaluate the advantages and disadvantages listed on the next few pages.

The Pros:

- **Ability to Choose the Funeral Home with the Right Personality.**

  As you know, your survivors will be working with the funeral home staff at a very emotional and stressful time, so it is important that you choose a funeral home that you believe they will be comfortable with.

- **Ability to Comparison Shop for Prices and Services**

  The costs of caskets and "professional services" vary dramatically. Obtain a detailed price list from the funeral homes you are considering, and take the time to compare your options to make an informed decision.

- **Protect Against Rising Costs**

  Negotiate a contract that allows the purchase of tomorrow's merchandise and services at today's prices. This refers to an option you may have to pre-pay for your casket and funeral services. This cost protection guarantee, however, may not be as simple as it appears. Read the funeral service contract carefully and if you are unsure about anything, ask questions. Also, each state has its own set of rules and regulations about how prepaid funeral expenses are handled. If you are unsure, call the state funeral directors association for more details. Choose a reputable funeral home and one with a long record of service to the community. If you don't know which funeral home to use, ask your friends and family for suggestions.

- **Shelter Funds**
  If necessary, funds can be placed in an irrevocable trust for Medicaid or estate planning purposes.

- **Obtain Peace of Mind**
  Knowing that you will be remembered exactly as you wish and ensuring that your loved ones will not be saddled with a heavy burden at a very vulnerable time will be a comfort to you today and as your time draws near.

The Cons:

- **Arrangements May Not Be Portable**
  You may not be able to shift your arrangements to a new location if you leave the state. Have the funeral home explain in their contract the boundaries of their service area and under what circumstances you can transfer the pre-need contract to another funeral home if you were to relocate or if the death were to occur outside of the service area.

- **Prices May Not Be Guaranteed**
  If a funeral home did not guarantee the prices of funeral costs and they inflate faster than the

growth of the deposit, you will be forced to substitute less expensive merchandise or provide additional funding. Make sure the contract guarantees that if the merchandise or services selected are not available at the time of need, merchandise or services of equal or greater value will be substituted at no extra cost.

If the prices are not guaranteed, the contract should explain who will be responsible for paying any additional amounts that may be due at the time of the funeral. In the case of leftover funds, ensure that they will be paid to your estate or else the mortician will probably keep them.

- **Penalties May Be Lurking**
  If a prepaid funeral contract is cancelled, you may get back less than you paid. Not all states require funeral directors to provide a 100 percent refund.

  Furthermore, if payment is structured in installments and payments are not completed before your death, the refund may be reduced by a sales charge which could be as high as 30 percent. Make sure cancellation penalties and refund policies are spelled out in the contract.

- **Costs Can Be Misunderstood**
  In many states, part or all of the interest earned on an account may be withdrawn each year by the seller as part of his administrative fees. Another typical misunderstanding is who will be responsible for paying taxes on the interest earned. Obtain a breakdown of all expenses in plain language and note in the contract who will be responsible for paying taxes on any income or interest generated by the invested funds.

- **The Funeral Home May Not Remain in Business or Have New Owners**
  We are currently seeing a lot of changes in the funeral service industry. Small, family-owned businesses are closing and/or selling to larger national firms. The wholesale funeral homes promising to save you thousands are moving into many cities. A very real concern for anyone pre-paying their arrangements is that the seller of those funeral services may not be in business at the time of your death or they may be under new ownership. Make sure that the pre-paid funds are secured and that the you or the account holder can withdraw them, if the funeral home goes out of business or changes hands.

- **Survivors May Not Know About the Arrangements**

  The specifics of your pre-paid funeral must be made known to family members, otherwise that money can be lost. Make sure your funeral details are put in writing and a copy of the plan is kept in a safe place along with your other important papers. You should inform a family member, close friend or even your attorney that pre-arrangements have been made, who they have been made with and where the documents are kept.

- **Funding May Be Irrevocable**

  Before accepting an irrevocable agreement, carefully consider the implications of your decision. Irrevocable agreements are helpful when eligibility for Supplemental Security Income (SSI), Medicaid or other public benefits are being determined, but they may limit flexibility. Many states now offer you the option of designating funeral accounts as irrevocable at a later date, should this protection be necessary.

  If Social Security benefits are not a primary concern, consider using a Totten Trust. This is an individual trust or savings plan earmarked for one's funeral. The consumer controls the account and can withdraw from it at any time. Usually a sum of money equal to today's funeral costs is deposited in a passbook savings, Certificate of Deposit (CD) or money market account, payable to a beneficiary of the account holder's choice. These funds are available immediately at the time of death without the delay of probate. Accumulated interest helps cover costs increased by inflation.

Another alternative is life insurance with an increasing death benefit equal to the cost of the funeral. Morticians usually expect to be named the beneficiary, but that choice is up to you. Keep in mind, however, that the choice you make may determine whether or not the funeral home will freeze the costs at today's prices.

In summary, pre-paying a funeral is a nice gesture but caution should be taken. Maintaining control of the funds and/or making certain they are protected are considerations of paramount importance.

The National Funeral Directors Association—www.NFDA.org—is an excellent source of information on this topic or, better yet, sit down with a trusted funeral director and talk about the pros and cons that apply to your unique situation.

■ Appoint Agent to Control Disposition of Remains

In some states, individuals are now able to legally assign an agent to control the disposition of their remains. Similar to a health care proxy or a living will, this legal document empowers the agent to make decisions on behalf of the individual—but specifically for taking care of the deceased's burial or cremation. In addition, the statute provides that an individual may give special directions, for example that they be cremated, that their body be buried in a particular grave at a specified cemetery, or that a particular funeral home handle the arrangements.

Appointing an agent to care for these matters is becoming popular for two reasons. First, even if a person's wishes are included in the will, an individual is usually buried or cremated long before a will is probated or even looked at. Second, with the increase of multiple marriages, same-sex relationships and individuals who are domestic partners, the disposition of a loved one's remains is increasingly being litigated. Be sure to check with your local funeral director for more details.

To-Do List

____ Draft or modify your will as needed.

____ Draft a living will or health care proxy to make your wishes for life-prolonging treatment known.

____ Adopt a durable Power of Attorney.

____ Consider pre-arranging your funeral.

____ Identify beneficiaries/owners whenever possible on insurance policies, retirement accounts, etc.

____ Consider putting individual into jointly-held accounts.

____ Consider crafting or reviewing your current estate plan.

____ Consider a Purposeful Trust™.

____ _____

____ _____

____ _____

____ _____

____ _____

Notes

Afterword

When Joanne died, I put my life on the shelf. For many months, life was consumed with the day-to-day details of her death. But slowly, I went back to work, began arranging social engagements and eventually introduced new people and new activities into my life, while still remaining close to Joanne's family and friends. When daily routine set in, the structure was a welcomed relief. I will never forget Joanne, but I have learned how to continue on with my life in a positive and life-affirming way.

After dealing with my grief and learning to adapt to a life different than the one I had hoped for, I have created a new life for myself. In 2003, I married Kathy, a wonderful woman who has brought light, laughter and a world of possibilities to my life. I am also proud to announce that I have been blessed with two children, my son Christopher and daughter Emily.

So, my final message to you is one of inspiration. Remember that while life may bring us unfair challenges from time to time, it can also bring unexpected blessings we never dreamed of.

Additional Resources

The following resources will be helpful to you in the event you need more information. To be sure of current numbers and addresses, please check the Internet.

American Bar Association
www.abanet.org

Career Gear (donations of men's clothing)
www.CareerGear.org

Department of Veterans Affairs
(800) 827-1000 or www.va.gov

Do Not Call Registry
www.donotcall.gov

Doctors Without Borders
www.DoctorsWithoutBorders.org

Dress for Success (donations of women's clothing)
www.DressforSuccess.org

Federal Trade Commission's ID Theft Hotline
(877) 438-4338 or www.consumer.gov/idtheft

Fraud Insurance
www.identityfraud.com or www.javelinstrategy.com

Funeral Consumers Alliance
www.funerals.org or 800-765-0107
Funeral Consumers Alliance is a nonprofit organization
dedicated to protecting a consumer's right to choose a
meaningful, dignified and affordable funeral.

Gift of Life Donation Initiative
www.organdonor.gov

The Grief Recovery Institute
(818) 907-9600 or www.grief.net
Offers an action program for moving beyond loss and a
great series of articles that can help you get a clearer
picture of what is true and accurate in relationship to
both grief and recovery.

Internal Revenue Service
(800) 829-1040 or www.IRS.gov

Mark Colgan, CFP®

585-419-2272 or 877-266-2233 or
www.colgancapital.com or www.planyourlegacy.com
Author, CEO and Founder of Plan Your Legacy and
President of Colgan Capital—an independent financial
services firm dedicated to providing custom financial
planning and money management services driven to
achieve life goals and leave a legacy of values and final
wishes.

National Funeral Directors Association
(414) 541-2500 or www.NFDA.org

National Self-Help Clearinghouse
(212) 840-1259
Provides information on variety of peer support groups.

Social Security Administration
(800) 772-1213 or (800) 325-0778 TTY or www.SSA.gov

Glossary

Administrator
A person appointed by the court to supervise the handling of an individual's estate in the event that no will has been executed.

Affidavit
Any written document in which the signer swears under oath before a notary public or someone authorized to take oaths (like a County Clerk), that the statements in the document are true.

Beneficiary
The named party who receives proceeds under an insurance policy, trust or will.

Bond
A debt security, similar to an I.O.U. When you purchase a bond, you are lending money to a government, municipality, corporation, federal agency or other entity known as the issuer.

Cash Value
The "savings element" in a permanent life insurance policy, which is the property of the policy owner.

Certificate of Deposit
A deposit with a specified maturity date and interest rate.

Certified Financial Planner
Anyone can call themselves a financial planner, but only those individuals who have voluntarily taken the extra step to demonstrate their professionalism and high ethical standards can be certified by the Certified Financial Planner Board of Standards. Their accreditation indicates they are capable in financial planning as well as managing a client's banking, estate, insurance, investment and tax affairs. Only those individuals can call themselves a Certified Financial Planner and use the CFP designation after their name.

Codicil
A document that amends a will. It must be executed like a will and witnessed by two people not named as beneficiaries for any of their assets.

Creditor
Lender of monies.

Death Benefit
The proceeds of the policy that will be paid upon insured's death.

Decedent
A person who has died. Also referred to as deceased.

Dependent parent
A parent who is determined to be dependent under I.R.S. standards and for whom an exemption can be claimed. See I.R.S. Publication 501 for more information.

Disclaimer
The refusal, rejection or renunciation of a claim, power or property.

Estate Tax
A tax paid on property or assets owned at the time of one's death.

Executor/Executrix
An individual appointed through a will to administer and distribute property upon the testator's death. Executor is the male version and executrix is the female form of the word.

Fiduciary
An individual who manages property or acts on behalf of another individual and is placed in a position of trust.

Guardian
An individual who has the legal right and duty to take care of another person or another's property because that person cannot legally handle these responsibilities.

Health Care Proxy (Health Care Power of Attorney)
A legal document that allows you to appoint someone to make medical decisions if you become unable to competently make them for yourself.

Interment
The act of burial.

Individual Retirement Account (IRA)
A retirement account that may have been established by an employed or self-employed individual.

Individual Retirement Account Rollover
A provision enabling a retiree or anyone receiving a lump-sum payment from pension, profit-sharing or salary reduction plan to transfer the amount into an IRA.

IRA Beneficiary Designation Account (IRA-BDA)
A retirement account established by a beneficiary. An inherited where the deceased's name remains on the account.

Intestate or Intestacy
The state of dying without a legal will where asset distribution is overseen by a probate court.

Irrevocable
Unable to be amended, altered or revoked.

Legacy
A combination of life facts, photos, video clips, favorite stories, powerful memories and wisdom that one can package together as a gift to future generations of one's family.

Medicaid
A joint federal and state program that helps with medical costs for people with low incomes and limited resources.

Medicare
The federal health insurance program for people 65 years and older. Certain people who are younger but who have disabilities and/or serious illness may also be eligible.

Living Trust
A legal arrangement, established during an individual's lifetime and which is fully amendable and revocable by its creator, under which a trustee holds title to property with the obligation to keep or use it for the benefit of the beneficiary. Living Trusts are commonly used as vehicles to avoid probate.

Living will
A legal document allowing you to express your wishes as to health care treatment, not estate planning. It makes clear what measures you want taken—or not taken—to keep you alive if you are seriously ill.

Mutual Fund
A financial intermediary that allows a group of investors to pool their money together under a fund manager who buys and sells securities with a predetermined investment objective.

Niche
A niche or "crypt" is a space in any structure for the interment of the remains of a human body.

Power of Attorney
A document that authorizes someone to act on another's behalf.

Power of Appointment
Typically used with trusts, it gives an individual the power to decide which beneficiaries receive distributions and in what amounts.

Principal
The total amount of money being borrowed or lent.

Probate
The process of proving that a will is genuine and distributing the property accordingly.

Roth IRA
A type of individual retirement account that allows contributors to make annual contributions and to withdraw the principal and earnings tax-free under certain conditions.

Stock Certificate
A document reflecting legal ownership of a specific number of stock shares in a corporation.

Testamentary Trust
A trust that is created upon the death of the decedent pursuant to the terms of the will through or as a result of the probate process.

Trust
A legal arrangement in which an individual holds title to property, subject to an obligation to keep or use it for the benefit of the beneficiary.

Trustee
A person who holds money or property for the benefit of another.

Supplemental Security Income (SSI)
Monthly benefits paid by the Social Security Administration to individuals who qualify because of limited income and resources or who are disabled, blind or age 65 or older.

Surrogate's Court
County or state court that handles cases involving the affairs of decedents, including administration of wills, estates and trusts.

Transfer Agent
Individual or institution that a company appoints to handle the ownership transfer of securities.

Transfer on Death (TOD)
The process of changing title of a security from one name to another upon the death of one of the titleholders.

Urn
Container designed to hold an individual's cremated remains.

Will
A legal document through which a person declares or designates how their possessions will pass after death.

Index

How to Order More!

If you found the knowledge, insight and experience in *The Survivor Assistance Handbook* helpful during a very hard time in your life, then perhaps you'd like to share the information with another friend, business associate or family member. Or pass the word to your doctors, hospice nurse, religious leader, funeral director, social worker, therapist and support group.

Call:
(585) 419-2272
Write:
Plan Your Legacy, LLC
179 Sully's Trail, Suite 301
Pittsford, NY 14534
Fax:
(585) 419-2265
Online:
www.planyourlegacy.com
Volume discounts available.

148

ABOUT THE AUTHOR

Mark Colgan is Founder and CEO of Plan Your Legacy and President of Colgan Capital. The combination of his personal and professional background gives him a unique perspective on financial and legacy planning. In 2001, he was a successful Certified Financial Planner™ professional who'd been married to his wife, Joanne, for seven years. When she died unexpectedly at the age of 28, Mark's wonderful life was dramatically changed forever.

Inspired by the challenges he faced as a young widower, Mark authored THE SURVIVOR ASSISTANCE HANDBOOK: A GUIDE FOR FINANCIAL TRANSITION. Mark also founded Plan Your Legacy, a company dedicated to helping individuals live and leave meaningful legacies by building legacy plans that reflect and preserve their values, life lessons, memories and final wishes.

Today, Mark is a national speaker and an often-cited expert on legacy planning. His articles have appeared in such national publications as U.S. News and World Report, The Journal of Financial Planning, American Association of Individual Investors, and Money Adviser, a Consumer Reports publication. He has also been cited by Fox News, CBS MarketWatch, Oprah and Friends, and other national media.

On a personal note, Mark and his current wife, Kathy, have two beautiful young children and reside in upstate New York.